SANTA MARIA PUBLIC LIBRARY

3 2113 00487 3975

D0578502

j 363.41

Rebman, Renée C., 1961-
Prohibition
c1999.

Discarded by
Santa Maria Library

Orcutt Br.   DEC 3 0 2002

BRANCH COPY

GAYLORD MG

Prohibition

Titles in the World History Series

WORLD HISTORY SERIES ■ ■ ■

Prohibition

by Renee C. Rebman

Lucent Books, P.O. Box 289011, San Diego, CA 92198-9011

*For my daughter, Scarlett, and
my son, Roddy*

Library of Congress Cataloging-in-Publication Data

Rebman, Renee C., 1961–
    Prohibition / by Renee C. Rebman.
        p. cm.—(World history series)
    Includes bibliographical references and index.
    Summary: Discusses Prohibition in the United States,
including why it was enacted, its effects on the people and
the nation, its connection with criminal activity, and its repeal.
    ISBN 1-56006-444-7   (lib. : alk. paper)
    1. Prohibition—United States—History—Juvenile
literature.   [1. Prohibition.]   I. Title. II. Series.
HV5089.R42   1999
363.4'1'097309042—dc21   98–34225
                                                    CIP
                                                    AC

Copyright 1999 by Lucent Books, Inc., P.O. Box 289011,
San Diego, California 92198-9011

Printed in the U.S.A.

No part of this book may be reproduced or used in any other
form or by any other means, electrical, mechanical, or otherwise, including, but not limited to, photocopy, recording, or
any information storage and retrieval system, without prior written permission from the publisher.

Contents

Foreword

Each year on the first day of school, nearly every history teacher faces the task of explaining why his or her students should study history. One logical answer to this question is that exploring what happened in our past explains how the things we often take for granted—our customs, ideas, and institutions—came to be. As statesman and historian Winston Churchill put it, "Every nation or group of nations has its own tale to tell. Knowledge of the trials and struggles is necessary to all who would comprehend the problems, perils, challenges, and opportunities which confront us today." Thus, a study of history puts modern ideas and institutions in perspective. For example, though the founders of the United States were talented and creative thinkers, they clearly did not invent the concept of democracy. Instead, they adapted some democratic ideas that had originated in ancient Greece and with which the Romans, the British, and others had experimented. An exploration of these cultures, then, reveals their very real connection to us through institutions that continue to shape our daily lives.

Another reason often given for studying history is the idea that lessons exist in the past from which contemporary societies can benefit and learn. This idea, although controversial, has always been an intriguing one for historians. Those who agree that society can benefit from the past often quote philosopher George Santayana's famous statement, "Those who cannot remember the past are condemned to repeat it." Historians who subscribe to Santayana's philosophy believe that, for example, studying the events that led up to the major world wars or other significant historical events would allow society to chart a different and more favorable course in the future.

Just as difficult as convincing students to realize the importance of studying history is the search for useful and interesting supplementary materials that present historical events in a context that can be easily understood. The volumes in Lucent Books' World History Series attempt to present a broad, balanced, and penetrating view of the march of history. Ancient Egypt's important wars and rulers, for example, are presented against the rich and colorful backdrop of Egyptian religious, social, and cultural developments. The series engages the reader by enhancing historical events with these cultural contexts. For example, in *Ancient Greece*, the text covers the role of women in that society. Slavery is discussed in *The Roman Empire*, as well as how slaves earned their freedom. The numerous and varied aspects of everyday life in these and other societies are explored in each volume of the series. Additionally, the series covers the major political, cultural, and philosophical ideas as the torch of civilization is passed from ancient Mesopotamia and Egypt, through Greece, Rome, Medieval Europe, and other world cultures, to the modern day.

The material in the series is formatted in a thorough, precise, and organized manner. Each volume offers the reader a comprehensive and clearly written overview of an important historical event or period. The topic under discussion is placed in a broad historical context. For example, *The Italian Renaissance* begins with a discussion of the High Middle Ages and the loss of central control that allowed certain Italian cities to develop artistically. The book ends by looking forward to the Reformation and interpreting the societal changes that grew out of the Renaissance. Thus, students are not only involved in an historical era, but also enveloped by the events leading up to that era and the events following it.

One important and unique feature in the World History Series is the primary and secondary source quotations that richly supplement each volume. These quotes are useful in a number of ways. First, they allow students access to sources they would not normally be exposed to because of the difficulty and obscurity of the original source. The quotations range from interesting anecdotes to farsighted cultural perspectives and are drawn from historical witnesses both past and present. Second, the quotes demonstrate how and where historians themselves derive their information on the past as they strive to reach a consensus on historical events. Lastly, all of the quotes are footnoted, familiarizing students with the citation process and allowing them to verify quotes and/or look up the original source if the quote piques their interest.

Finally, the books in the World History Series provide a detailed launching point for further research. Each book contains a bibliography specifically geared toward student research. A second, annotated bibliography introduces students to all the sources the author consulted when compiling the book. A chronology of important dates gives students an overview, at a glance, of the topic covered. Where applicable, a glossary of terms is included.

In short, the series is designed not only to acquaint readers with the basics of history, but also to make them aware that their lives are a part of an ongoing human saga. Perhaps they will then come to the same realization as famed historian Arnold Toynbee. In his monumental work, *A Study of History*, he wrote about becoming aware of history flowing through him in a mighty current, and of his own life "welling like a wave in the flow of this vast tide."

Important Dates in the History of Prohibition

| 1874 | 1900 | 1919 | 1920 | 1925 | 1929 | 1933 |

1874
The Woman's Christian Temperance Union is formed

1900
Carry Nation begins her temperance crusade

1919
January: The Eighteenth Amendment is ratified

October 28: The Volstead Act is passed by Congress

1920
January 29: Prohibition begins

November 2: Warren G. Harding is elected twenty-ninth president

1925
Al Capone takes charge of the Torrio gang

A woman rings in the new year with her hidden flask of alcohol in this 1925 photograph.

1929
February 14: The St. Valentine's Day massacre takes place in Chicago

June: The Women's Organization for National Prohibition Reform is formed

1933
February: The Twenty-first Amendment is passed

April 7: Beer is legal once more

December 5: Prohibition ends

A Nation Divided

President Herbert Hoover called Prohibition "a noble experiment."[1] It was an experiment destined to fail. Prohibition, the Eighteenth Amendment to the U.S. Constitution, outlawed the manufacture, transportation, and sale of alcoholic beverages in the United States. It was in effect for nearly fourteen years, from January 29, 1920, to December 5, 1933. The amendment pitted the "wets," Americans who denounced the act as an infringement of their rights and who were determined to keep drinking, against the "drys," those determined to see the law enforced. The conflict was waged against a backdrop of dramatic social and economic change.

Paradoxically, in light of the intent of the Eighteenth Amendment, the 1920s was an era of good times. World War I was over, and the nation wanted to celebrate. There was an eagerness to break old rules, defy tradition, and enjoy life. Victorian morals and a rigid code of properly sedate behavior were out—flappers, bobbed hair, jazz music, and automobiles set the tone for what was to become a decade-long party.

Returning soldiers pounded the pavement for jobs, eager to make good money and to spend it. Women, for the first time in American history, had won the right to vote in 1920. A strong sense of freedom and independence underpinned a general chafing

During the 1920s, traditional, strict behavioral codes gave way to a new, fun-loving spirit characterized by jazz music and energetic dances, such as the Charleston (pictured).

at the restrictions of Prohibition. People were not about to conform to the restrictions of Prohibition. From the beginning, the issue was hotly contested by housewives, politicians, and everyone in between.

Billy Sunday, the most famous evangelist of the time, gave his strong support to Prohibition, declaring,

The reign of tears is over. The slums will soon only be a memory. We will turn our prisons into factories and our jails into storehouses and corncribs. Men will walk upright now, women will smile, and the children will laugh. Hell will be forever for rent.[2]

Prohibition, many believed, would cure the country's problems. Working men would no longer spend their paychecks at saloons, and factories would not experience loss of labor due to drunkenness. But its effects were quite different. Organized crime flourished. Bootleggers became rich almost overnight. Speakeasies sprang up in basements and behind drugstores in towns, small and large, across the nation. Rum-running, a dangerous and lucrative new business, was rampant. A huge supply of illegal liquor made its way across the border from Canada.

Billy Sunday, an evangelist who strongly supported Prohibition, believed temperance would rid the United States of problems like crime and poverty.

In fact, Canadian lawmakers had previously passed temperance laws in that country, but with many loopholes, leaving enforcement up to individual counties and municipalities. These laws had been repealed after World War I with an exception that prohibited the sale or export of liquor to countries where Prohibition was legally in force, a provision blatantly ignored by those willing to take chances and make a fast buck. The border was difficult to patrol, and rumrunners were continually busy plying their trade. They had no shortage of anxious customers; the consumption of alcohol was a socially, if not legally, acceptable pastime.

Prohibition affected everyone. The temptation of the illicit led many an honest citizen to indulge in drinking, and many tolerated the practice as a harmless vice in others. Officeholders campaigning for re-election faced the political impossibility of courting constituents so split over the issue.

Perhaps the single weakest aspect of Prohibition was its enforcement. Though the federal government recruited a huge force of agents, the job required no qualifications beyond a simple endorsement from a congressman or prominent local authority. Turnover was high; the average length of service was only a few months. Many agents had criminal records, and corruption in the forces was widespread. Agents were often simply dismissed for serious infractions that should have been prosecuted.

Unwilling to concede failure, the government welcomed the support of influential businessmen whose opinions were widely publicized. Henry Ford remained a staunch supporter of Prohibition, claiming he would be through with manufacturing if booze came back to the country. The

Speaking Out

Many influential businessmen of the 1920s took a vocal stand on the Prohibition issue, helping to fuel the fire of conflict. Henry Ford stood strong on the side of Prohibition. As quoted in Edward Behr's Prohibition: Thirteen Years That Changed America, *his reasons are laid out in a no nonsense approach.*

"For myself, if booze ever comes back to the U.S. I am through with manufacturing. I would not be bothered with the problem of handling over 200,000 men and trying to pay them wages which saloons would take away from them. I wouldn't be interested in putting autos into the hands of a generation soggy with drink.

With booze in control we can count on only two or three effective days' work a week in the factory—and that would destroy the short day and the five-day week which sober industry has introduced. When men were drunk two or three days a week, industry had to have a ten- or twelve-hour day and a seven-day week. With sobriety the working man can have an eight-hour day and a five-day week with the same or greater pay. . . . I would not be able to build a car that will run 200,000 miles if booze were around, because I wouldn't have accurate workmen. To make these machines requires that men increase their skill."

famous automaker declared he "would not be bothered with the problem of handling over 200,000 men and trying to pay them wages which saloons would take away from them."[3] Many others agreed; the industrial revolution created an unprecedented demand for employees capable of operating complicated machinery, and employers could not afford the risk of dealing with workers who drank.

Midway through the era, statistics continued to mock the Prohibition effort. In 1927, states that maintained records reported a 317 percent increase in deaths from alcoholism over 1920. In 518 communities, allowing for the increase in population, arrests for drunkenness increased more than 125 percent.

The "noble experiment" finally failed when the cry for repeal succeeded in 1933. In the midst of a terrible depression, a majority of the population decided that if people were going to pay money for booze, no matter what, they might as well pay it to the government, which would return it to the community in one form or another. Prohibition was ended. Alcohol was heavily taxed, but legal, and speakeasies and rumrunners began to disappear. The wild era of the Roaring Twenties was over, but Prohibition's legacy of controversy, corruption, and crime echoed across the country for years to come.

1 The Roots of Prohibition

The demand for national prohibition was firmly in place for many years before the Eighteenth Amendment was ratified and took effect in 1920 as part of sweeping social change during the latter half of the 1800s. The industrial revolution was in full swing, accompanied by waves of immigration and widespread urbanization in America. The urban saloon filled with immigrants and other working-class men became a common fixture during this time. Competent, reliable workers were needed to keep many new industries and factory lines running, and critics of alcohol embarked on a moral crusade to persuade Americans that the economy and social fabric were threatened by its corrupting influence.

William Windom, for many years a U.S. senator, delivered a speech in 1887 describing conditions he had observed:

> The saloon creates a demand where none before existed that it may profit by supplying that demand. It artificially stimulates an evil habit that it may thrive by pandering to it. It methodically breeds debauchery, poverty, anarchy, and crime for pay. . . . Experience indicates that four-fifths of American drinking and drunkenness is due in the first instance not to any natural appetite

of our people, but to the presence and sleepless efforts of this gigantic enginery, working seven days a week and twenty-four hours a day, unrestrained by any scruple and everywhere contemptuous of public and private right.[4]

Women Take Charge

Women's temperance unions and hundreds of church temperance leagues led the battle cry in nearly every city across the country. Official unions had been organized as early as 1873. The most famous, formed in 1874, was the Woman's Christian Temperance Union, led by Frances E. Willard. Her efforts to banish alcohol were tireless. Speaking at the 1884 Republican National Convention, she stated, "I come on behalf of millions of women . . . to ask that the guarantees and safeguards of law shall be stripped from the saloons of my country . . . and that the land we love may at once and forever go out of partnership with the liquor traffic."[5]

There was also a strong prohibition movement building on college campuses, with organizations forming in 146 colleges by 1893. Protests took place during many rallies and political conventions, attended

Joining the Crusade

In How Dry We Were: Prohibition Revisited, *Henry Lee describes the day Frances E. Willard, famed leader of the Woman's Christian Temperance Union, felt compelled to join the crusade against alcohol. The incident and her reaction demonstrates the crusader's fervor.*

"It was in 1874 on Market Street, Pittsburgh, at Sheffner's, an old-fashioned saloon with a high, heavily-corniced bar, fauceted barrels of whiskey, sawdust-strewn floors and a few round tables with chairs. For a year, the determined local ladies had been demonstrating by ranging themselves on the curbstones outside saloons, singing such appropriate hymns as 'Jesus the Water of Life Will Give' and kneeling in prayer 'on the cold, moist pavement.' For the most part, the saloon keepers and their patrons accepted the noise philosophically, but Sheffner was too polite. The day that Frances Willard happened to go slumming with the girls, he allowed them inside. The leader placed her Bible on the bar, read a Psalm, briskly rendered 'Rock of Ages' and then courteously invited the neophyte Frances to do the praying.

'It was strange, perhaps, but I felt not the least reluctance,' she remembered long afterwards, 'and kneeling on that sawdust floor, with a group of earnest hearts around me and behind them, filling every corner and extended out into the street, a crowd of unwashed, unkempt, hard-looking drinking men, I was conscious that perhaps never in my life save beside my sister Mary's dying bed had I prayed as truly as I did then. This was my crusade baptism. The next day I went on to the west and within a week had been made president of the Chicago W.C.T.U.' "

Frances Elizabeth Willard led the Woman's Christian Temperance Union in its fight to banish alcohol.

Women's temperance unions such as this one would visit saloons and ask the owners to shut down their businesses. The groups often took matters into their own hands, smashing kegs and bottles of alcohol in these establishments.

by students and the general public. But it was women who battled in the forefront. Often carrying axes and hatchets, visitation committees actually went to saloons to beg saloonkeepers to abandon their business, appealing that they "desist from this ruinous traffic that our husbands and brothers, and especially our sons, be no longer exposed to this terrible temptation."[6] Typically, women would then go about methodically breaking open beer kegs, shattering bottles of liquor, and destroying as much stock as possible. The war against "demon rum" was personal; many women had suffered abuse from alcoholic husbands and lived in poverty when their men spent hard-earned wages at the saloon.

The effects of these raids were temporary, however. Saloons were forced to close but soon reopened to brisk business. The conflict escalated between wets and drys as immigrants continued to patronize saloons.

A One-Woman Army

Carry Nation, a tall, formidable Kansan, was perhaps the most famous foe of alcohol. Her first husband had died of the effects of alcoholism after repeated failed attempts to reform him. She later remarried, but the experience left her determined to see alcohol banned, and at the

Carry Nation, shown here with her infamous hatchet in one hand and her Bible in the other, felt divinely inspired to destroy saloons and usher in temperance.

fender. When she visited saloons, she often went alone. Armed with a hatchet, she was bent on causing as much destruction as she could. Crying, "Smash! Smash! Smash! For the love of Jesus, Smash!"[7] she broke up furniture, bottles, and anything else she could get her hands on before she was thrown out. News reporters followed her everywhere, recording her activities. Some saloons hired extra guards in anticipation of her arrival. Many actually welcomed the publicity her visits would bring; publicity guaranteed more patrons would visit their establishment just to see and hear what transpired.

Local authorities were at a loss as to how to handle the situation. Carry was illegally destroying property, but property connected with morally objectionable and sometimes officially sanctioned activity. Public opinion was generally on her side. Consequently, Carry rarely spent more than one night in jail. She used her incarceration as an opportunity to garner even more publicity by posing for photographers. Clutching her Bible, she would kneel on the floor of her cell and pray aloud as the press crowded around her.

Her eccentric and energetic efforts ended shortly after the turn of the century when illness forced her to give up traveling, and she died in a mental institution in 1911. Her name remains synonymous with the temperance movement, and her unforgettable antics have earned her a place in Prohibition history.

The Time Is Ripe

Newspaper coverage of the mounting war against drink escalated. The temperance

age of fifty-three she set out on a personal crusade. Some states at that time were dry and actively enforcing their own prohibition laws. Liquor was officially illegal in her home state, yet saloons still existed, ignored by local authorities. This random and spotty success against evil drink was not enough for Carry; she brought to her crusade an unparalleled sense of mission.

Attacking saloons in Kansas at first, she soon spread her message to many other states. She was much in demand as a lecturer and published newsletters entitled *Smasher's Mail, Hatchet,* and *Home De-*

crusade was bolstered by the press. With public opinion swinging rapidly for nationwide prohibition, industrial leaders rallied together in support of the cause. The country was in the midst of the industrial revolution. Goods were being mass-produced faster and in greater variety than ever before. Competition for consumer dollars was fierce, and image was important. It made political and economic good sense to support what was becoming a very popular movement.

And the safety factor could not be ignored. Machinery used in transportation and industry was now more complex, more powerful, and much more dangerous to operate. Employers believed it was imperative that the workforce have clear heads and steady hands. Accidents were commonplace in the factories, and some-

times fatal. Automaker Henry Ford went so far as to insist his workers be teetotalers. He hired a private police force to spy on them. Anyone caught buying alcohol more than once was fired.

The alcohol problem was debated by the National Safety Council at their 1914 annual meeting. At the conclusion of the discussion, the conference unanimously adopted the following resolution:

Whereas it is recognized that the drinking of alcoholic stimulants is productive of a heavy percentage of accidents, and of diseases affecting the safety and efficiency of workmen; therefore, be it

Resolved, that it is in the sense of this round-table meeting at the third annual congress of the National Safety

---

The View of the Press

Quoted in The Amazing Story of Repeal, *by Fletcher Dobyns, the New York* Tribune *gave this harsh account of liquor traffic in the March 2, 1884, issue, which blames nearly all of society's ills on alcohol.*

"It is impossible to examine any subject connected with the progress, the civilization, the physical well-being, the religious condition of the masses, without encountering this monstrous evil. It is the center of all social and political mischief. It paralyzes beneficent energies in every direction. It neutralizes educational agencies. It silences the voice of religion. It baffles penal reform. It obstructs political reform. It rears aloft a mass of evilly inspired power which at every salient point threatens social and national advance; which gives to ignorance and vice a greater potency than intelligence and virtue command; which deprives the poor of the advantages of modern progress; which debauches and degrades millions, brutalizing and soddening them below the plane of healthy savagery."

Council, that it places itself on record as being in favor of eliminating the use of intoxicants in the industries of the nation.[8]

The endorsement of the National Safety Council pushed the movement forward. Activists were mainly middle-class citizens, businessmen, and crusading women who believed success would depend on convincing the working class, largely immigrant patrons of the saloons that Prohibition would be to their benefit. This flawed strategy intensified class distinctions, however, and engendered as much resentment as support.

The vast numbers of immigrants flooding into the United States primarily from northern and eastern Europe did not understand what the uproar was about. Euro-pean attitudes toward alcohol consumption were, and had always been, much more re-laxed. German beers, Irish whiskeys, and Italian wines were basic beverages in those countries. Nearly all the thriving breweries in the United States were owned by Germans. The United States Brewers' Association was the focus of much debate all over the country; many hoped that even if prohibition went through, the beer trade would be exempt. Teetotalers, however, were adamant in their all-or-nothing position. Wets and drys boycotted each other's businesses, and street brawls often broke out.

The controversy raged on. By the end of World War I in 1918, liquor producers and politicians from wet communities were the only major opponents of Prohibition left. In the general moral climate, demon rum was losing the fight. The new

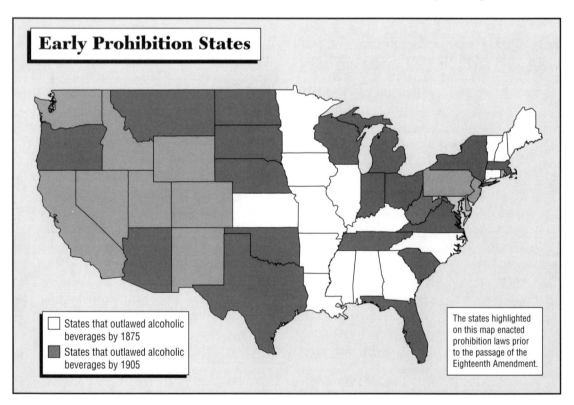

Early Prohibition States

☐ States that outlawed alcoholic beverages by 1875

■ States that outlawed alcoholic beverages by 1905

The states highlighted on this map enacted prohibition laws prior to the passage of the Eighteenth Amendment.

Saloons such as this one were the focus of much protest from industrial leaders. Employers feared that workers who frequented these saloons raised the rate of accidents, disease, and unproductiveness in the workplace.

authority and power of women helped turn the tide. A half century of campaigning for the cause had not been in vain.

At the same time, the nation was welcoming thousands of young men returning from victory overseas. With the war over, citizens feared that money previously funneled toward the war effort would be pumped back into the saloons. Activists played on these fears, pressuring politicians at the local and state levels.

The Eighteenth Amendment was adopted by Congress in August 1917 with the requirement that it be ratified by the necessary thirty-six states within seven years. President Woodrow Wilson vetoed it on constitutional and ethical grounds, stating, "In all matters having to do with personal habits and customs of large numbers of our people we must be certain that the established processes of legal change are followed."[9] Congress overrode the veto, however, and the act became law. Ratification occurred in January 1919.

Wayne Wheeler's Contribution

On October 28, 1919, Congress passed the National Prohibition Act, more commonly known as the Volstead Act, which specified just how the amendment would be enforced. The Volstead Act, named for Minnesota congressman Andrew J. Volstead, who introduced it in the House of Representatives, was actually drafted by Wayne Wheeler. Wheeler was the powerful and manipulative leader of the Anti-Saloon League. A native of rural Ohio, Wheeler had suffered a terrible accident in his

Teetotalers

The interesting origin of the term teetotaler *is explained in Daniel Cohen's* Prohibition: America Makes Alcohol Illegal. *As far back as Civil War times, small groups of women working for the temperance cause kept careful records of their membership in notebooks and often made detailed lists of men caught drinking in saloons.*

"The word 'prohibition' was not used or even thought of at that time. But 'temperance' is a misleading description, for it implies moderation in drinking alcohol. The early temperance societies did not demand that their members completely give up all alcohol. But within a few years tolerance for even moderate drinking completely disappeared. The pioneer American Temperance Society pledged new members to total abstinence, marking their names on the membership list with a T for 'total.' That is how the word 'teetotaler,' one who is opposed to all alcoholic drinks, came into the language. Though a variety of antiliquor organizations continued to use the word 'temperance' in their name, they were in reality 'teetotal' in outlook."

youth when a drunken farmhand working for his father rammed a pitchfork into his leg. His hatred for alcohol was intense.

Wheeler worked his way through college and became a lawyer. Politics fascinated him. He maintained a card index system on public officials, noting their political views and their private scandals, and was one of the most feared lobbyists in Washington. His successful, behind-the-scenes campaigning helped make his home state of Ohio one of the driest in the Union. By 1908, fifty-seven of its eighty-eight counties had gone dry under county local option laws.

Wheeler was not above using scare tactics to advance his cause. With America in the midst of World War I, Wheeler used the opportunity to discredit the nation's German citizens when he wrote the following to Custodian of Alien Property A. Mitchell Palmer:

> I am informed that there are a number of breweries around the country which are owned in part by alien enemies. It is reported to me that the Anheuser-Busch Company and some of the Milwaukee companies are largely controlled by alien Germans. . . . Have you made an investigation? [10]

Wheeler handpicked Andrew J. Volstead to introduce the Prohibition bill he had written, considering him a pliant supporter who could be directed at will. Volstead was not a well-known or a particularly dynamic politician. Neither was he a strong advocate of the Prohibition movement, but he did support it as political good sense and oversaw its ratification to the end.

The Prohibition Commission

John F. Kramer of Mansfield, Ohio, was appointed the first commissioner of Prohibition. Kramer described his organization in the January 11, 1920, edition of the *New York Times:*

> The machinery will consist of two branches. One branch will operate in the States as units, the other in districts of which there will be 10 in the United States. . . . In each there will be a Federal Prohibition Director. Under each Director there will be inspectors. . . . At the head of each of the 10 districts there will be a prohibition agent. Under each prohibition agent will be a staff of men. . . . All these men will be experienced in police and secret service duties. They will have particular charge of the discovery of illicit sale and illicit manufacture of intoxicating liquors. They will make raids and arrests.[11]

The Volstead Act did exempt specific kinds of distilled or fermented products, including certain patent medicines, doctor's prescriptions, sacramental wine, syrups, vinegar, and cider. Brewers could remain in business if they produced "near beer" with a maximum of 0.5 percent alcohol. (Beer normally contained as much as 3.7 percent alcohol.) Penalties for improper use were to be fines and prison terms. Officials braced themselves for January 17, 1920, when the law was to take effect, and America began stocking up.

Private Supplies Readied

People believed it would be legal to store private supplies of liquor in warehouses

Bar patrons raise their glasses to propose a final toast on the eve of Prohibition. Many Americans began to stockpile liquor before the Volstead Act took effect, even building warehouses to store their supplies.

and safety deposit vaults. Those with the money to do so built up huge private stocks. On January 16, one day before the deadline, a federal judge ruled that all liquor not actually in a person's home would be subject to seizure. There was a mad scramble all over the country as people rushed to reposition their supplies.

Saloons and liquor dealers held last-minute, cut-rate sales. Many nightclubs held elaborate mock funerals featuring coffins for the deceased "John Barleycorn," a traditional effigy symbolizing liquor. One wealthy client of the Park Avenue Hotel in New York City gave a huge private party where everyone wore black, black caviar was served, and drinks came in specially ordered black glasses. The night before the Volstead Act took effect, reporters walked the streets of major cities looking for excitement and sensational news stories. But, other than a few parties, things were relatively quiet. John Barleycorn expired with a whimper instead of a bang.

The Winners Celebrate

The following day was a cause for celebration for the activists and supporters of Prohibition. Extravagant rallies included celebrities, politicians, and parades. Endless speeches were made extolling success. In Washington, D.C., a rally was attended by hundreds of congressmen, the entire Anti-Saloon League, and thousands of well-wishers. Secretary of State William Jennings Bryan was jubilant in his praise for the effort that toppled the liquor industry:

> They are dead, that sought the child's life. They are dead! They are dead! King Alcohol has slain more children than Herod ever did. The revolution that rocked the foundation of the Republic will be felt all over the earth. As we grow better and stronger through the good influence of Prohibition, we will be in a position to give greater aid to the world.[12]

Prohibitionists celebrated victory: What had seemed an impossible task had been accomplished. America was dry. But though the battle may have been won, the war had just begun. One of the few hard-headed realists who saw this was former president William Howard Taft. Those who thought that "an era of clear thinking and clean living" was at hand were living in a fool's paradise, he wrote. The law had been passed "against the views and practices of a majority of people in many large cities. . . . The business of manufacturing alcohol, liquor and beer will go out of the hands of law-abiding members of the community and will be transferred to the quasi-criminal classes."[13] He would be proven right time and time again as the Roaring Twenties started to roar.

Chapter

2 "Tell 'em Joe Sent You"

With Prohibition in place, the thirsty country looked for alternate sources of liquor. The most obvious and immediate result of Prohibition was the proliferation of speakeasies, which sprang up in cities large and small, rich and poor. Speakeasies were private alcohol-serving clubs that often used legitimate businesses as a front for the illegal activity, so-called as members were cautioned to "speak easy" about the secret locations. Many were small operations hidden in basements or the backrooms of drugstores and hardware stores, but many speakeasies in the larger cities were spacious, glamorous nightclubs, often patronized by a wealthy clientele.

Liquor by the Brick

In New York, liquor by the brick was a popular—and legal—purchase. The salesperson gave careful instructions on how to handle the brick so as not to let it ferment. The instructions, of course, were meant to help the customer achieve exactly the opposite result. In How Dry We Were *by Henry Lee, a saleswoman's demonstration is related step by step.*

"A port brick and a gallon glass jug on the counter in front of her, she explained briskly.

You dissolve the brick in a gallon of water, and it is ready to be used immediately.

Do not place the liquid in this jug and then put it away in the cupboard for twenty-one days because then it would turn into wine.

Do not stop the bottle with this cork containing this patented red rubber siphon hose because that is necessary only when fermentation is going on.

Do not put the end of the tube into a glass of water because that helps to make the fermenting liquor tasty and potable.

Do not shake the bottle once a day because that makes the liquor work."

A speakeasy customer is eyed through a peephole as he knocks on the door of the club. Admittance to the elusive speakeasies was often a complicated, secretive process.

A speakeasy might occupy a penthouse, a Wall Street office building, or a brownstone rooming house; one on the East Side of New York was set up to look like a synagogue. Tenants of a busy street dotted with "clubs" often posted a sign on their door declaring No Speakeasy in hopes of avoiding late-night interruptions by would-be customers looking for a quick drink.

In fact, during the dry era, thirty-two thousand speakeasies replaced the fifteen thousand legal drinking places of pre-Prohibition New York. Bishop James Cannon Jr. of Virginia, a supporter of total abstinence, deplored the soaking-wet metropolis as "literally Satan's seat."[14]

New York speakeasies became the stuff of legend. Getting into one was a compli-cated task. Intricate series of ringing bells, doors with sliding panels, and admittance cards, or code phrases such as "Joe Sent Me,"[15] were all necessary steps to obtaining entrance. Some speakeasies maintained several different addresses by constructing multiple entrances, all leading to the same club, yards apart from each other on the same street. This ruse allowed them to stay in continuous operation. Even if federal agents issued an order to padlock a certain address, the club owners simply directed patrons to the next door down, thus re-maining literally one step ahead of the law.

Inside the Doors

Once inside, the patron experienced an atmosphere of camaraderie. In the better clubs, good food was available as well as liquor, all overpriced. Sometimes live music was provided and dancing chorus girls put on a show. But even the quieter clubs were popular and filled to capacity. The *New York Times* rationalized the success of the new nightlife scene, which Prohibition spawned by the closing of traditional saloons:

> The answer has been a group of cafes that call themselves clubs—although technically they have no more right to the name than has the Waldorf-Astoria. But the very name "club" is a part of the general scheme of surrounding patrons with the psychology of privacy and intimacy—which psychology has had no small factor in ousting the clammy dread of the law that had placed its damper on Broadway's spirits since July 1919.

The very architecture of the new places is a part of the propaganda. The successful "club" is full of booths and alcoves and cozy wall benches, which somehow contribute to the atmosphere of "just us, members."[16]

Running a speakeasy was profitable but costly. One New York proprietor reported his costs at $1,370 a month, including more than $400 in "hush money" to Prohibition agents, the police department, and district attorneys. Hush money guaranteed the owner that authorities would look the other way and play dumb about the illegal activity that went on in the speakeasy. The cop on the beat also received $40 to turn his back each time liquor supplies were being delivered.

Women in the Business

Women as well as men recognized substantial profits were to be made by engaging in the risky speakeasy business. One of the most famous female speakeasy owners was Texas Guinan, a rowdy blonde as well known for her personality as her establishment. She greeted her customers with a loud, sassy "Hello, Sucker!"[17] and plied them with as much liquor as they could drink—and pay for. Her net earnings during one ten-month period totaled $700,000. Federal agents often raided her business, and Texas herself would be escorted to the paddy wagon, smiling and waving good-bye to her customers, promising to be open for business again soon.

Getting into a Speakeasy

Speakeasies became very popular, and the showmanship of the owners added glamour and excitement to their patrons' visits. In The Lawless Decade *by Paul Sann, a* New York Times *reporter gives an example of how admittance was gained.*

"The intricate and mysterious rites observed before patrons are allowed to enter seem to be chiefly intended to add romantic excitement to the adventure, since authorities are not likely to remain long unaware of their existence. Introduction by someone who has been there before is usually required. Then there is the business of registering the new patron's name and perhaps the issuing of a card of admittance to be presented on the next visit. It is sometimes made even more important looking by a signature or a cabalistic sign on the back of the card. Many persons about town carry a dozen or more such cards.

The devious means employed to protect the entrances to speakeasies probably adds to the general mystification. Bells are to be rung in a special way. A sliding panel behind an iron grill opens to reveal a cautious face examining the arrivals."

And she kept her promise, even if she was forced to find a new location. Her customers faithfully followed her.

Another famous female proprietor was Helen Morgan. Customers flocked to drink liquor and hear the talented owner sing the blues and sad torch songs while perched atop a piano. After acquitting the well-liked and well-respected Morgan of a liquor charge in court, one juror remarked, "We couldn't take the word of two Prohibition agents against Miss Morgan."[18]

Helen retired from the speakeasy trade by the end of the twenties, blaming wear and tear on her nerves, but the good quality of her product and her singing helped glamorize the legacy of the speakeasy.

Women were not just running the speakeasies, they were patronizing them in great numbers. Prohibition introduced one unforgettable phenomenon of the Roaring Twenties, the flapper. Distinguished by her bobbed hair, short skirts, garter belt (often dressed up with a flask of "hooch"), and penchant for parties and the Charleston dance step, the flapper took the nation by storm.

Saloons had traditionally been regarded as a men's only retreat, but the new speakeasy welcomed the flapper into the fold. Wearing evening finery, women stopped in with their escorts after dinner or the theater at all hours of the night. They behaved as equals by drinking and smoking cigarettes in public. The flapper heartily believed the words of a popular song of the day, "Ain't We Got Fun?" She was determined to enjoy herself.

Flappers were not the only women frequenting the speakeasies. Prostitution was

Texas Guinan (left) owned her own speakeasy, taking full advantage of the profits to be made. Another speakeasy owner, Helen Morgan (right), also performed at her club, singing the blues to her faithful customers.

a continual problem. The police in larger cities reported street trade had diminished as the prostitutes went underground, operating from the speakeasies with fewer risks. Many of the owners actually paid the girls to do business from the clubs, employing them as "hat check girls" and "hostesses" for lonely patrons. The prostitutes were seldom bothered by the local police as long as they did business quietly, and the federal agents raiding the club to confiscate alcohol were much too busy and overworked to care.

Women and drink were plentiful commodities in the speakeasies. If Prohibition made the flapper bloom, it also gave birth to the so-called cocktail, as mixed drinks became the rage. More a necessity than a fad, the cocktail was invented to disguise the awful taste of so-called bathtub gin, and the flavored wood alcohol the bootleggers sold. Quantity was favored over quality and use of inferior ingredients was commonplace. Home brew did not taste any better. Everyone, or so it seemed, was making bootleg liquor, whether for resale or their own consumption. The process was fairly simple.

Speakeasies had many women customers, including the flapper (pictured), who drank and smoked with as much zeal as her male counterparts.

Home Brew

Beer was often made in a tub if a more sophisticated brewing apparatus was not available. One home brewer recalls the method used:

The procedure necessitated peeling enough potatoes to more than cover the bottom of a bathtub, dumping potatoes and peels alike into the tub and permitting the mess to ferment for days. Sugar, yeast and water were added at appropriate times in appropriate amounts till the tub was half filled.

Eventually, the concoction, now bubbling dangerously close to the tub brim, was drained off in those old-fashioned blue bottles which had rubber stoppers and clamp-on porcelain tops. During the long-drawn-out process, of course, no baths could be taken.[19]

Bathtub gin was brewed in great amounts because the ingredients were easy to acquire. It consisted of pure grain alcohol, glycerine, juniper juice, and water.

Moonshine, White Lightning, Bathtub Gin, and Rotgut

Prohibition alcohol had many names. The Sirs Digest, *Spring 1996 issue, explains why the term* rotgut *was perhaps the most descriptive of all.*

"Perhaps the most accurate name for this illegal whiskey was 'rotgut.' Bootleg whiskey was often distilled under incredibly unsanitary conditions by 'chemists' who sometimes—either mistakenly or knowingly—used toxic ingredients. In 1927 alone, nearly 12,000 people died from drinking poisoned alcohol. Thousands more were permanently injured. Because ethyl alcohol, used in whiskey production, was outlawed by Prohibition, bootleggers often used methyl alcohol as a substitute. A tiny droplet of methyl alcohol can be fatal if ingested. Methyl alcohol also damages the nerve cells of the eye's retina, so that even if the victim survives, blindness can result."

A Prohibition agent dumps confiscated moonshine. Such bootleg whiskey sometimes contained lethal doses of methyl alcohol.

Another common but dangerous drink was known as "needle beer." Near beer with less than 0.5 percent alcohol was purchased legally and opened, then shot with a syringe of pure alcohol before drinking to increase its concentration. Miscalculation of the amount of alcohol injected could render the beer lethal. Many people drank needle beer and diligently continued doctoring home brew to try and improve the taste no matter how sick they became after consuming it.

Home brewing was so common by the end of the second year of Prohibition that the Woman's Christian Temperance Union conducted a "Star in the Window" campaign. Members urged every home owner and businessman who did not use liquor to display a blue flag with a white star in the center along with the message, "We are

Americans. We Support the Constitution."[20] The number of homes participating were fewer than hoped for. From the home basement to the speakeasy, liquor, whatever the quality, flowed like water.

For Medicinal Purposes Only

The Volstead Act had determined that alcohol used for medicinal purposes would be legal; as an unintended consequence, doctors prescribed it and druggists dispensed it at incredible rates. More than a million gallons of "medicinal" comfort was sold each year. This legal excess was ignored by Prohibition agents, leaving doctors, druggists, and their patients to enjoy the scheme guilt free.

Another scheme of using medicinal and industrial alcohol legally was masterminded by George Remus, the wealthiest and perhaps most clever bootlegger of all. Remus, knowing Prohibition was soon to take effect, used all his life savings to buy up whiskey certificates and distilleries. As a lawyer, Remus knew the Volstead exemptions were ironclad and he manipulated them to his advantage. The certificates allowed him to operate within the boundaries of the law. His alcohol was slated for medicinal and industrial use only and he had the right to sell it. What happened to the alcohol after it left his hands was not his concern. Remus cornered the market by becoming owner of the largest distilleries in America. He filtered the alcohol through drug companies he bought and duly bottled some for medicine, but most of it went to bootleggers, speakeasy owners, and exclusive private clientele. Remus kept a good eye on his books, jostled numbers as needed, and made millions.

Men like Remus were Prohibition agents' biggest targets. Arresting customers or speakeasy owners did not stop liquor at its source; it was the bootleggers the agents wanted. Information had to be gathered on their whereabouts and contacts, and the agents sometimes used primitive surveillance techniques to do so. Wire-linked microphones were built into lampshades at speakeasies and monitored around the clock by stenographers working in shifts. This method did net the agents some arrests from information overheard, but clients of the speakeasies soon found out about the operations and deliberately spread misinformation to thwart the efforts of the agents. They

A 1927 photo shows bootlegger George Remus in jail. Before he was caught by agents, Remus tried to get around Prohibition laws by selling alcohol for purported medicinal use.

intentionally named well-known politicians, clergymen, and even high-ranking Prohibition agents themselves as participants in bootleg traffic.

Izzy and Moe

Two Prohibition agents working as a team did manage to make arrests in record numbers, reporting a total of 4,392 during their five-year career. Isadore Einstein and Moe Smith (known as Izzy and Moe) would stop at nothing to get the job done. Often dressing in women's clothes or impersonating street cleaners, tourists, or working-class stiffs to infiltrate speakeasies, their antics were outrageous but successful. Once Izzy even impersonated himself, telling a bartender, "I'm Izzy Einstein,

Izzy Einstein and Moe Smith raid a distillery. Izzy and Moe's impressive arrest record was due to their unorthodox methods such as impersonating tourists, street cleaners, and even dressing as women to infiltrate speakeasies.

the Prohibition agent."[21] The bartender merely laughed, served him a drink, and was arrested.

Although criticized constantly by their superiors for their unorthodox methods, Izzy and Moe were popular with the public and the press. As their popularity spread, jealousy set in among high-ranking agents, and in 1925 both men were fired. No other Prohibition agents ever came close to such an impressive arrest record and no others were as well known or loved. Izzy and Moe seemed to make a dismal, thankless occupation fun. And the public, caught up in a whirlwind of Prohibition madness, appreciated them.

The Public Wants to Drink

The capitalist lesson of supply and demand was never more clear than during the Prohibition era. The public demanded alcohol and supply grew to meet the demand. Prohibition agents worked against insurmountable odds. Customers, speakeasy owners, bootleggers, and corrupt public officials and prosecutors banded together to keep the liquor trade operating. The obvious failure of the Volstead Act to keep alcohol from Americans caused even diehard Prohibitionists to reexamine their viewpoint.

Pierre du Pont of the Du Pont chemical firm had been an advocate of Prohibition until 1926. At that point he changed his views and publicly supported the Association Against the Prohibition Amendment (AAPA). The AAPA had been formed in 1919, before the Volstead Act had taken effect. Early in the 1920s it continued its opposition to Prohibition with even stronger dedication. Du Pont's published view of the issue seemed to echo the feelings of many Americans:

> I have never yet found anyone who has been able to tell me satisfactorily why selling over the bar is objectionable. The principal argument seems to be that the bartender is an informal host who keeps people drinking. For myself, I see no objections to a bar.[22]

The number of speakeasies continued to grow, despite the efforts of the incorruptible government agents. Influential businessmen and celebrities were wooed by the speakeasies, which gained status with their patronage. Proprietors were known to turn away ordinary customers or relegate them to back tables in order to seat famous patrons at the best and most visible locations. Snob appeal generated a lot of business. Once the word got around that society types were patronizing a club, people clamored to get inside. Rubbing shoulders with the wealthy and well known was all part of the fun.

The demand for liquor, and a pleasant place in which to enjoy it, guaranteed the speakeasy would be in operation for the duration of Prohibition. Public opinion seemed to have changed soon after the Eighteenth Amendment took effect. Postwar moral standards were less rigid. The new freedoms being experienced by the public were embraced and enjoyed to the fullest degree. Drinking became an ac-

The number of speakeasies began to increase as the demand for liquor rose and drinking became an accepted habit for both men and women.

cepted feature of social life for both men and women. The speakeasy helped glamorize the lure of alcohol and changed the lifestyle of an entire generation.

3 Rumrunners

During Prohibition liquor made its way from foreign countries across all American borders. Booze was legal nearly everywhere else in the world. From Cuba, the Caribbean, and Mexico millions of gallons of rum and other liquors were smuggled either across land or by boats heading up the coast. American Prohibition vastly improved economic conditions in small villages that had previously depended on fishing as their major commerce. The demand for bootleg liquor was a boon to their livelihood. The fishermen made a much higher profit using their boats for rum-running than for fishing, and they were happy to engage in the illegal activity to improve their standard of living. In California, Oregon, and Washington State shipments were received daily. The Pacific Coast of the United States was less closely monitored than the Atlantic. Still, rum-running could be very risky on either coast.

The Atlantic Coast was a hotbed of activity, particularly along the border from Boston to New York. Countries such as Scotland, Germany, and France sent huge

A secret door reveals a hidden compartment in this truckload of lumber. Prohibition agents in Los Angeles discovered seventy cases of scotch concealed inside.

Smuggling liquor to the United States from other countries was a profitable but risky business. Here, a captured Canadian rum-running boat is relieved of its cargo in New York in 1931.

shipments of high-priced liquor across the Atlantic Ocean. So many boats waited in line in international waters just off the coast of New York City to make their connections that the route became known as Rum Row. Though smugglers were known generally as rumrunners, their illegal cargo included more than just rum. Whiskey, scotch, vodka, gin, and champagne were all in demand and delivered on a regular basis.

To stay in the competition, Americans manufacturing their own bootleg liquor turned to whiskey certificates to keep their supplies circulating to customers. It was perfectly legal to export liquor intended for medicinal use to other countries. The certificates allowed them to maintain brisk production and the fiction of legality. The truth was that the liquor was never intended to leave the States. Hundreds of thousands of gallons would be purchased by foreign businessmen—on paper only.

Roy Haynes of the Prohibition Commission wrote the following:

> If we believed the tales of all who apply for liquor permits, we would naturally come to the absurd conclusion that the whole world is sick and desperately in need of distilled spirits. . . . Does anyone believe that Scotland, home of whiskey, is really in need of 66,000 gallons of American whiskey for non-beverage purposes? . . . It is the irony of ironies, a wet world, come to dry America to beg for liquor.[23]

Canadian Liquor

More liquor was imported to the United States from Canada than anywhere else. Canadian producers and rumrunners worked together amicably throughout Prohibition to quench Americans' thirst. The

Canadian border, at 3,986 miles long, offered both temptation and opportunity to the rumrunner. Alcohol was smuggled across unpatrolled stretches of land. The federal government underestimated the force of men needed to patrol both land and sea borders. Border patrols were woefully inadequate and rumrunners worked day and night.

Earlier prohibition efforts had failed miserably in Canada and all prohibition laws had been repealed there by the end of World War I. Liquor production was back in full force. Pleas from the United States to Canadian officials to restrict alcohol manufacturing went unheeded. In fact, with the new demand for liquor from the now dry United States, manufacturing increased rapidly and dramatically.

Canadian statistics also indicated a startling rise in alcohol exports to other foreign countries. U.S. officials knew that liquor specified for export actually made its way to America, but the paper trail was impossible to follow or monitor.

Canadian whiskey was in such demand that one bootlegger operating out of Pittsburgh increased the prices his homemade bootleg brought simply by pasting fake Canadian labels on his bottles.

Smuggling, on a small or large scale, could not be stopped. The various ways the alcohol was transported set new standards for stealth, ingenuity, and downright gutsiness.

Crossing the Great Lakes

The Great Lakes provided easy access to major cities, in Michigan, Ohio, and New York, that were waiting eagerly for Canadian bootleg.

Some individuals smuggled alcohol under their coats, as this young woman reveals. Others hid liquor in their hats, sleeves, or specially constructed pants pockets.

Rumrunners' vessels and pleasure boats filled with tourists picking up private stock choked the waterways. Boats crossed back and forth continually. Tourists could only smuggle as much as they could conceal from customs officials; they carried bottles in their hats, up coat sleeves, in specially constructed pants pockets, in belts concealed under dresses, wherever they could hide it and still manage to walk without making clanking noises.

One man smuggled his contraband liquor across the border concealed in his daughter's baby buggy:

I used to do it all the time—smuggle booze that is—I'd take my daughter over . . . in her pram. But underneath her, there was a false floor and I'd put the bottles in there. Then I'd give her a sucker, and off we'd go. And just as we got to Customs, I'd pull the sucker out of her mouth, and she'd howl. The Customs man, not wanting to put up with a screaming baby would just look at me and say, "Get out of here." And off we'd go. And of course, as soon as we were through, I'd give her another sucker.[24]

Individual citizens smuggled many bottles of alcohol past customs in various ways, but the true rumrunner depended on a high-volume business to make his profits. Boats of every size and specification—steamers, tugboats, motorboats, sailboats, and rowboats, were used to smuggle bootleg. As much liquor as possible was loaded into them on every run. Canadian whiskey was bound up in burlap bags. Whiskey imported from Scotland came in wooden cases. Burlap bags had distinct advantages and were preferred by rumrunners for two reasons. The bags took up less room and were easier to load into small irregular spaces. Also, in case the boat was being chased by the Coast Guard and whiskey had to be thrown overboard, the bags would sink. The wooden cases merely became floating evidence.

Alcohol was also transported by air. Private aircraft was hired by organized gang bootleggers who needed big supplies on a daily basis. The landing strips were mainly farmers' fields, whose owners were well paid for their trouble and often assisted the pilots during landing. For a nighttime landing, the farmers would drive their trucks to the field and keep their lights on. They would also set small fires to guide the aircraft. Some farmers earned as much in one day of rum-running as they would in harvesting a season's crop. Aerial rum-running was profitable for everyone involved.

Across the Ice

A winter crossing of the Great Lakes was a more difficult proposition, but the determined rumrunner did not let bad weather stop him. Old jalopies were used to haul the liquor over the frozen ice. The cars were purchased cheaply, for five to ten dollars, so if one fell through the ice, the rumrunner did not lose much money. Small boats were sometimes rigged on top of skids or runners and hauled behind the cars to transport even more cases of alcohol. The driver left his door open so he could jump out if necessary.

One rumrunner recalled a night he made four trips to transport eight hundred cases for the big-time bootlegger George Remus:

It was no problem taking it across the ice. The ice was safe. I made four trips in my truck. Where the channel was open, I built a bridge over it . . . and I'd just drive over the bridge. This channel was like a big crack in the ice. Some days it would be open . . . some days closed. We took eighteen foot planks and put them one over the top of each other, you see. Then, you hammer a spike through, into the ice so it won't slip. Then you go on it, see, and it would grab the ice. Then we added another eighteen foot plank on top of it. So when you go over with the truck,

Bootleg in the Air

Bootleg whiskey made its way from Canada by boat, jalopy, strapped under clothing, and by air. In his book Rumrunners, *C. H. Gervais explains how the latter worked.*

"Air rumrunning was perhaps the most dynamic of them all. Aerial smuggling was a novelty, and at first it was something that went unhampered by authorities, who already had their hands full in trying to combat convoys of boats that sneaked across the river at all hours of the day and night.

The aerial rumrunners were big-time and gang-organized, under contract. Al Capone and the Purple Gang were lucratively involved in this, since they needed swift supplies on a daily basis. It was estimated that as much as $100,000 worth of booze left Windsor and neighboring parts each month for American landing strips.

In Ontario [Canada] the landing strips were farmers' fields, given over to the rumrunners at a flat rate fee. Sometimes they were paid as much in one day as what they would have earned if they had put in a crop. Sometimes farmers aided the runners by assisting the pilots in landing at night. They would drive their cars to the field and keep their lights on, and often would set up lanterns and build small fires. For this assistance, they were paid as much as $5 a case."

A 1930 photo shows a rum-running plane. Gangsters found aerial rum-running to be an efficient method to transport alcohol.

it went down so far into the water . . . it dipped into the channel and the water would come up to the truck. Well we'd go across, unload the whiskey and have fifteen minutes to drive back. We did that quite a few times.[25]

Rum-Running at Sea

Rumrunners working off the Atlantic Coast took different and sometimes much more dangerous risks. They often faced gunplay from the Coast Guard, piracy, and even mutiny from disgruntled crew members. The rumrunner at sea achieved a sort of dubious folk hero status. The lure of the business was powerful, and not simply for the opportunity to make money. Many smugglers had been in the navy during World War I. They knew and loved the sea. Rum-running offered them a chance to experience some exciting action again. As one rumrunner nostalgically told a writer for *Popular Boating* magazine: "If drinking the stuff was half as much fun as running it in was, then I can understand the drunkard's problem."[26]

Colorful stories of the rumrunners abounded. One famous rumrunner was a woman known as Spanish Marie. She assumed command of her husband's boat after his untimely demise; he and the ship's captain had fallen overboard in a drunken stupor after sampling some of the ship's cargo. It was rumored that Marie gave them a push. She renamed the boat *Kid Boots* and took over her late husband's crew and clientele. It was to her advantage to be intimidating in the rough business of rum-running, and she acted and dressed the part. According to historian Edward Behr,

Prohibition agents reveal bottles of liquor seized from a coal steamer in New York Harbor.

she strutted about with a revolver strapped to her waist, a big knife stuck in her belt and a red bandanna tied around her head. Legend had it that she was about as tough as she looked. She was captured in March 1928 while unloading liquor at Coconut Grove, and was released on five hundred dollars bail on the plea that she must take care of her babies. The bail was increased to $3,500 when investigators found the children at home with a nurse and Spanish Marie at a speakeasy.[27]

Another well-known rumrunner was Captain Bill McCoy. He was not a drinking

Bootleg Travels in Style

In Edward Behr's Prohibition: Thirteen Years That Changed America, *Sally Rand, a famous fan dancer, recalls the yachts that bootleggers purchased after the stock market crash of 1929. The luxury boats were then used to transport booze.*

"These beautiful yachts that cost half a million dollars were sitting around (on the West Coast) with barnacles on them. These are the people who jumped out windows. Who's gonna buy a yacht? A man came up to me and said, 'Hey, are any of these yachts for sale?' I said: 'Are you kidding? They're all for sale.' The guy was a bootlegger. So I sold the half-million-dollar yachts to bootleggers. For five or ten thousand dollars. And took my six percent commission on them. Beautiful.

The bootleggers decorated them with pretty girls in bathing suits, like going out for a little sail. Load up and come back.

. . . The interiors were done in rosewood, gold handles on the toilets and all that jazz, great oil paintings in the salons. They're now jammed up with loads and loads of wet alcohol . . . the interiors of them were gutted and ruined."

man and got involved with rum-running from his intense love of sailing. His boat, the *Arethusa*, was better equipped and better run than any other bootlegging boat. His crew was loyal, he paid them very well, and he allowed no drinking on board. His motto was We Do Business Day and Night.[28]

The *Arethusa* was equipped with shelves of liquor available for sampling by prospective buyers, but only two buyers were allowed on board at a time, a policy meant to deter a possible hijacking. A large machine gun was also placed prominently on deck to discourage any trouble.

The Coast Guard finally caught up with the *Arethusa* in November 1924. Rather than risk losing his boat when she was fired on, McCoy surrendered and was jailed.

Despite the illegal nature of his business, Captain Bill McCoy was known for his fair dealings and high-quality liquor. The origin of the phrase "the real McCoy," meaning genuine and on the level, has been attributed to the rum-running of Bill McCoy.

Pirates

One of the most vicious and deadly threats to a rumrunner was pirates. The illegal cargo of alcohol was not usually of interest to the pirating ship; its main objective was the profits of the rumrunners. Typically pirates would lie in wait until all the alcohol had been sold, then board the rumrunner's ship in a surprise attack, rob the rumrunners of the money that had just been collected, and kill the crew if necessary. Pirates usually crippled the ship's engines before leaving to avoid pursuit from anyone left alive or anyone boarding the ship later.

Coast Guard patrols became used to finding crippled ships floating aimlessly, manned by injured crewmen and bodies or totally unmanned if the victims had been dumped overboard. In these cases, identifying the vanished crew was impossible unless the bodies happened to wash ashore. A rumrunner's fear of pirates was far greater than the threat of the inadequately manned Coast Guard.

Carry Nation's Navy

The task of combating rumrunners on inland waterways such as the Great Lakes and along coasts fell to the Coast Guard. For thirteen years, the fleet took part in the country's longest naval engagement, nicknamed "Carry Nation's Navy."[29] Considering the magnitude of the assignment, the Coast Guard deserved far more credit than was given for the role it played.

At the start of Prohibition, smuggling bootleg in from the sea was a small operation, but it soon grew to immense proportions. It quickly became evident that the Coast Guard needed more men to combat the increasing number of rumrunners. By 1924 Congress authorized the addition of 550 temporary Coast Guard officers to augment the force of 2,240 enlisted men. Recruiting posters went up in post offices across the nation, enticing young men to join: "U.S. Coast Guard requires men of action who like adventure; a chance for advancement; one year enlistment."[30]

Coast Guard patrols also faced the problem of rum-running boats that were much faster than their own, a handicap

Coast Guard officers survey a captured rum-running vessel stocked with cases of alcohol. Prohibition prompted such an increase in smuggling that the Coast Guard's staff was not enough to keep up with the deluge.

that made successful pursuit impossible. The rumrunners, backed by wealthy bootleggers, used specially built boats manufactured in discreet workshops in New York City and other places up and down the coast. The boats featured bulletproof windshields, armor plating, and storage for up to four hundred cases of bootleg and could travel at thirty-five knots.

One motor mechanic named Jimmy McGhee constructed a speedboat for bootleggers that consisted of a floating platform powered by twin water-cooled airplane engines, which he purchased cheaply from stocks of World War I surplus. His boat was capable of speeds up to sixty-five miles an hour, far faster than the fastest Coast Guard boats.

Cracking Secret Codes

Many smugglers' boats were equipped with radios, used to communicate with land bases in sophisticated code. Coast Guard analysts played a cat-and-mouse game of intercepting radio frequencies and attempting to crack the codes to foil the delivery of goods before smugglers could improve their methods. One of the biggest bootlegging conglomerates, the Consolidated Exporters'

Piracy

Piracy was a far greater threat to rumrunners working off the coasts than antismuggling crafts. An account of one unfortunate boat that had probably been raided and was found by the Coast Guard is given in Rum War at Sea *by Malcolm F. Willoughby.*

"Grim evidence of foul play appeared soon afterward. A fog hung heavy over Vineyard Sound, and coast guardsmen of the Gay Head Lifeboat Station heard faint sounds of whistles and bells coming over the water. As the fog lifted momentarily, they saw a steamer which was awash. When the men started to launch their boats to go to her assistance, the vessel rolled over, her boilers exploded, and she went down. This steamer was the 150-foot *John Dwight* out of Newport. The men made an extensive search but found no trace of the crew. It was presumed at the time that the crew had left in their own boats, but these could not be found. The next day, eight bodies with life preservers were discovered floating in Vineyard Sound amid barrels of bottled ale. The bodies were all cut and mutilated, giving rise to the theory that the men might have had a battle with pirates or a fight among themselves. The answers to this riddle and what caused *John Dwight* to sink were never known."

Bootleggers were extremely ingenious in hiding their loot. On this schooner, 3,000 cases of liquor were concealed under a load of lumber.

Company, hired a retired British Royal Navy expert to devise and change its code every few weeks, paying him a $10,000 retainer.

Elizabeth Smith Friedman, a senior cryptanalyst for the Coast Guard, testified against Consolidated Exporters' Company in court. She gave an example of their encoded instructions: "Anchored in harbor. Where and when are you sending fuel?" became: "MJFAK ZYWKH QATYT JSL QATS QSYGX OGTB."[31]

At Friedman's insistence, the federal government developed the CG-210, a Coast Guard patrol boat packed with high-frequency receivers and direction finders and staffed with cryptanalysts that could listen in on a large number of coded messages simultaneously. It was a high-tech breakthrough that proved immensely use-ful during World War II. Knowledge gained through the CG-210 operation aided cryptanalysts in decoding messages from Germany and Japan.

False Flags and the Three-Mile Limit

Any vessel flying the American flag could be legally stopped and searched by the Coast Guard, so many ships flew under British flags to avoid searches and obtained legal clearance papers claiming their cargo was headed for foreign ports. Their cargo was, of course, headed to the States. To further confuse matters, ships' names were changed frequently.

The Coast Guard After Prohibition

The Coast Guard played an important part in Prohibition enforcement but was fighting a losing battle. However, the skills acquired in the process greatly helped the Coast Guard later, as is explained by Malcolm F. Willoughby in Rum War at Sea.

"The press was mixed; while the Coast Guard received a 'good press' in many quarters, it was by no means good in others. The Service did not enjoy popularity with either wets or drys; the wets criticized it, of course, because it was carrying on a campaign against the rumrunners; the drys criticized it since it did not completely stop the flow of liquor from the sea. It was a cross which the coast guardsmen had to bear, and [they] bore it well.

But many good things for the Coast Guard came out of these 14 years of rum warfare. The Service was greatly expanded, and while it became reduced at the end of the period, it remained larger and more important than it had been previously. Instead of a service known for the most part locally along the coast, it became internationally known. Much of the experience gained by its personnel was immensely valuable. Its 'esprit de corps' was immeasurably enhanced and that enhancement has persisted down throughout the years. Intelligence became highly developed and has remained so. Standardization of communications procedures in line with those of the Navy was a strong plus factor in World War II."

Liquor was hidden on board in very ingenious ways. A search of one schooner, hauled in off the coast of Long Island Sound, yielded 5,538 bottles. Officials were about to end the search when a concrete floor aroused suspicion; its removal uncovered another 1,200 bottles. A second concrete floor was then also removed, revealing 1,350 more bottles. The additional cargo had nearly escaped detection. The vessel was in excellent condition and the Coast Guard took it over for use in its fleet.

Another problem facing the Coast Guard was the three-mile limit beyond which foreign ships could not be seized. This gave the ships plenty of open sea in which to make plans, contact their land bases, and wait for the proper opportunity to slip through to the shore. In 1923 the limit was extended to twelve miles in an effort to boost the Coast Guard's effectiveness. Ships were thus relegated much farther out and in rougher waters, and the run into shore was much longer, increasing chances of detection and pursuit. Crews on a ship being pursued would often dump their cargo, set the vessel on fire, and abandon it in a desperate attempt to avoid arrest.

To obtain advance information on deliveries, Prohibition agents paid informants two dollars a day, a tactic that sometimes backfired when informants sent the Coast Guard on a wild goose chase to intercept a decoy boat filled with cheap methyl alcohol while another boat delivered the real whiskey farther down the coast.

Another method of tricking the Coast Guard involved sending out fake distress signals, then ambushing the Coast Guard boat when it arrived to take care of the call, mocking the true mission of the Coast Guard, nearly forgotten in the Prohibition era, which was to ensure the safety of ships at sea and rescue vessels in distress.

Corrupt Customs Officers and Guardsmen

The Coast Guard was not untouched by corruption. Many of its officers were offered and accepted kickbacks from rumrunners in exchange for unhindered passage to shore. Some were favored with a personal supply of liquor fresh off the boats. The officers and guardsmen would keep what they needed to drink and sell the rest for profit.

Canadian officials observed some of this underhanded activity from the Canadian shore of the Detroit River. Bad faith, sparked by the smuggling problem, brewed constantly between the United States and Canada during Prohibition. The United States accused Canada of ignoring Prohibition and making no effort to stop smugglers from exporting liquor across the border. Canadian officials suggested the United States should take a look in their own backyard for illegal activity before placing the blame elsewhere. Canadian minister of national revue William D. Euler did not hesitate to point out Coast Guard corruption when he testified before the House of Commons on May 21, 1929:

> I took the trouble last fall to go down to Windsor. . . . I could see the United States Customs office on the other shore, and I could also see that it was not difficult to detect any boats that left the Canadian shore to go to the American side. . . . I got into conversation with a man engaged in the business of exporting liquor. I asked him, "Do you cross in the daytime?" He answered, "Yes, quite often." I said, "How is it they do not get you?" He replied with a smile, "It just happens that they are not there when we go across." [32]

While some corruption was certain, for the most part, Coast Guard officials were diligent and honest in their battle with the rumrunners. Outnumbered and unpopular, they did their jobs in the face of statistics proving the rumrunners enjoyed far more success than they; the Coast Guard's rate of interception never rose much above 5 percent. Their inability to succeed was scoffed at by many. Although the Coast Guard may not have won the rum wars, it did gain invaluable experience, develop improved standardization of communications, expand its services, and become internationally known. It became recognized as a viable resource, continued to improve upon its reputation, and is a solid and respected division of the armed services of the United States today.

4 Chicago: Corruption, Crime, and Capone

Even before the onset of Prohibition, when organized crime gained a strong foothold, corruption, crime, politics, and liquor were firmly intertwined in the city of Chicago. Gangs had nurtured various profitable rackets for years, including bootlegging, gambling, prostitution, protection, and strike breaking. The very term *racket* came into common use during the twenties as gang activity proliferated. A racket is defined as "any scheme by which human parasites graft themselves upon and live by the industry of others, maintaining their hold by intimidation, force and terrorism."[33]

Voting in Chicago

Organized crime in the 1920s was often protected by crooked politicians who directly or indirectly thwarted police intervention in the gangsters' activities in exchange for the gangsters' promise of support in the next election, usually in the form of stuffed ballot boxes. Crooked election boards were common in Chicago, and multiple voting occurred in nearly every election.

Chicago's political bosses also promised jobs to voters who backed favored candidates. "Big Bill" Thompson first cam-

William Hale Thompson (left), newly-elected mayor of Chicago, is sworn into office in 1914. "Big Bill" vowed to "clean up the dirt of the rotten administration in power." His most supportive campaigners, however, were gangsters.

paigned for mayor of Chicago in 1914 and served several terms until 1923. One of Thompson's mentors, Fred Lundin, used the promise of jobs to successfully round up votes for Thompson. He worked the streets, lining up local "street captains" and election agents, and passing out cards to be filled in with the names of likely Thompson voters: "On each card was a space for a notation of what kind of job the precinct captain wanted in case of victory."[34]

"Big Bill" gave many speeches vowing to eliminate corruption in Chicago. "I am going to clean up the dirt of the rotten administration in power," he promised. "No policeman will be sent to the cabbage patch if he offends some politician; not while Bill Thompson is your mayor."[35] His sentiments appeared well intentioned, but his most ardent and active campaigners were all gangsters.

Thompson also realized the value of a wet platform in a city populated by 600,000 beer-drinking German immigrants. Their support, along with an endorsement from the saloon and liquor lobby, boosted Thompson to victory.

Strikebreaking for Profit

Strikebreaking was another racket profiting organized gangs. Chicago in the 1920s was a growing industrial city; conditions in its factories were often poor, and workers tolerated low pay and long hours. A nationwide labor movement reached organizers in Chicago aimed at improving working conditions, and trade unions grew.

The unions examined working conditions and pay scales, then made demands for change to factory management. If the demands were not met, the union would call for a strike. During a strike, employees refused to work. Factory management would be forced to meet demands or face a shutdown, production delays, and financial losses.

Management would often turn to gangsters to break the strike by violent attacks on union leaders and strikers. In the wake of such intimidation, many strikes were broken, and employees in fear for their lives returned to work.

But gangsters exploited their usefulness further, demanding more and more money from management to keep things under control. This form of blackmail was effective. The factories either paid the gangsters or faced future shutdowns if unions gained strength. Strikebreaking was an extremely lucrative racket.

For their part, unions also hired thugs to defend themselves, resulting in criminal influence and control of both the management side and labor unions.

In practice, organized crime involvement did not depend on an invitation from labor or management. Gangsters would simply muscle in on any business they felt was profitable and demand "protection" money—for protection from the gangsters themselves. Businessmen paid on a continuing monthly basis simply for the privilege of being left alone. Those who did not ran the risk of losing their business to arson and other violence.

Other Profitable Rackets

Gangsters were also involved in the prostitution racket, protected from raids for the most part by policemen on the take and corrupt politicians. Prostitution rackets went hand in hand with the many speakeasies controlled by gang leaders. Prostitutes operated from these safe havens with the gangsters taking the major portion of all money they earned.

Gambling was another racket that earned huge amounts of money. Gangsters ran numbers games, similar to an illegal lottery, where chances were sold on a winning ticket worth varying amounts. Money was collected on a daily basis from hundreds of people that liked to play the numbers.

Betting was another form of gambling that gangsters took part in. Bets were taken on various athletic events, such as boxing matches, that were often fixed with a predetermined outcome designed for the gangsters' benefit. Profits collected on losing bets could be enormous, and gangsters and athletes could win more by losing on purpose than by an honest victory.

The Vice Problem Investigated

The power of organized crime became so pervasive that the Illinois Association for Criminal Justice launched an extensive investigation of causes and conditions of crime within the state. A lengthy report issued in 1926 stated some of its findings on crime in Chicago, particularly as related to Prohibition:

> Organized crime is not, as many think, a recent phenomenon in Chicago. A study of vice, crime, and gambling during the last twenty-five years shows the existence of crime and vice gangs during that period and how they have become more and more highly organized and powerful. . . . Bombing, combined with window smashing, slugging and shooting, has become a profession practiced by specialized crews or gangs. . . . A study of over three hundred cases of

bombings in the last quarter-century seems to justify the following classification by motive: gambling wars, "black hand," political bombings, interracial conflict, labor union ("direct action"), and merchant association ("racketeering"). . . . Within organized gambling, however, many of the characters and all the patterns of violence and anarchic warfare have been developed. . . .

> Finally, with the coming of prohibition, the personnel of organized vice took the lead in the systematic organization of this new and profitable field of exploitation. All the experience gained by years of struggle against reformers and concealed agreements with politicians was brought into service in organizing the production and distribution of beer and whisky.[36]

Modern technology also enabled organized crime to grow. Automobiles, telephones, and machine guns helped gangsters expand their criminal empires over entire regions. Improved communications meant rackets could be run more efficiently. Violence escalated as modern weaponry was used to terrorize victims and rival gang members. Crime was run as a business. The modern conveniences needed to run that business cost money. Thanks to Prohibition, bootlegging provided a steady source of income for gangsters.

The Appeal of Organized Crime

Bootlegging was supported by both the upper and lower classes. The upper classes needed bootleggers to supply their liquor.

This 1931 photo shows the captured rumrunner "Baboon" in Philadelphia, its deck piled with 1,000 sacks of liquor. During Prohibition, organized crime quickly staked its claim in the bootlegging business.

The Wickersham Commission, established by President Hoover in 1930 to provide yet another report on the problems of Prohibition, found that whereas many citizens were concerned about bootlegging, many more rationalized the practice and patronized criminals providing the service:

> It is all a reflection on the social mind. We seek by law to tell the people you can not do so and so, when the people are not in that frame of mind. . . . They want their liquor. They do not care what chances the other fellow takes so long as they don't take the chance.[37]

The lower classes engaged in bootlegging to make a decent living, setting aside ethical considerations and considering bootlegging a trade much like any other trade. The urban lower classes comprised mostly recent immigrants who were struggling to achieve the American dream of prosperity. To the poor Italians, Slavs, and Irish, bootleggers were neighborhood heroes. Their prestige and power were envied. The Italian gangs were the strongest in Chicago. Fellow Italians felt a certain degree of national pride in their material success, and support of bootlegging operations was widespread in ethnic communities.

The Big Bosses

The two most powerful gangsters in Chicago before Prohibition were Big Jim Colosimo and John Torrio. Colosimo began his career as a petty pickpocket, then became manager of a brothel, and eventually made millions. His headquarters, Colosimo's Café, was a favorite gathering place for celebrities and society notables. Big Jim wanted someone he could trust to run his brothels so he could spend more time with his elite clientele at the café. In 1909 he sent for his nephew from Brooklyn, John Torrio.

Torrio proved himself by making the brothels even more successful. He also earned a reputation for ruthlessness. When extortionists tried to muscle in on his business, he lured them into traps and murdered them. Recognizing that Prohibition was soon to become a certainty, he approached his uncle about getting into the bootlegging racket. Colosimo, satisfied with the money his vice business was earning, was not interested. It was a major point of conflict with Torrio, who quietly continued making plans.

In 1919, Torrio imported a young criminal from Brooklyn, Al Capone, into his organization. Capone learned the ropes and became Torrio's number-one aide. With Capone under his wing, Torrio felt ready to make his move.

On May 11, 1920, Torrio arranged for his uncle to wait at the café to receive a large shipment of whiskey. Colosimo entered the café and was still inside the vestibule when an unknown gunman sprang from the coatroom and shot him twice. Colosimo died instantly.

Police were never able to conclusively identify the hitman or to prove the hitman

James "Big Jim" Colosimo, seen here with his wife Dale Winter, made a fortune running the brothels of Chicago. His reluctance to get involved in bootlegging cost him his life and set the stage for the rise of Al Capone.

had acted on Torrio's orders. Torrio took over his uncle's gang with Capone at his side. The decade of the most notorious crime spree in Chicago was about to begin.

Torrio's Short Career at the Top

John Torrio enjoyed five years at the top of his game as leader of the toughest gang in Chicago. He became known as "the Brain" because of his organizational skills and cold logic. He was the first man to try and truly organize crime throughout the entire city. His plan was to bring all gangs

(Polish, Irish, and Italian) under one confederation and split up the city into sections, allotting portions to each gang. The gangs would agree to operate only in their own sections, but gang wars would often break out over territorial lines that had been crossed.

Hitmen and gang henchmen murdered leaders of other gangs over bootleg that had been peddled inside their territory. Many men died. Elaborate funerals drawing crowds of mourners were commonplace. The caskets were ornate, and multitudes of floral arrangements were sent to the church, the biggest arrangements purchased by the gang that had arranged for the murder of the deceased.

Torrio's reign ended when a brewery deal turned sour. Irish gang leader Dion O'Banion sold Torrio his brewery for a half-million dollars. Torrio was happy to acquire a facility certain to increase bootlegging profits. A week after O'Banion collected his money, however, federal agents raided the brewery and seized everything. Torrio realized he had been swindled and vowed revenge. O'Banion was gunned down inside the flower shop he ran.

In retaliation, attempts were made by the O'Banion gang on Torrio's life. On January 24, 1925, Torrio was ambushed in front of his apartment building. Hit by several bullets, he hovered near death for more than a week but eventually recovered.

Torrio, now aged forty-three, decided he had had enough. He turned the reins over to Capone, declaring, "It's all yours, Al. I've retired."[38] Torrio enjoyed his ill-gotten wealth for many years, finally dying of a heart attack at the age of seventy-five.

John Torrio (center), Jim Colosimo's nephew and heir. After a brief reign of five years, and an attempt on his life, he turned control of his criminal organization over to Al Capone.

Good Guy, Bad Guy

Al Capone was a popular figure with the general public. He was free with money and often gave to the poor to enhance his image. Because Prohibition laws were so unpopular, those who broke them were not thought of as criminals, even criminals as dangerous as Capone. His rationalization of his work as quoted in Time-Life Books This Fabulous Century *explains his view, a view that more than a few agreed with.*

"Everybody calls me a racketeer. I call myself a businessman. When I sell liquor, it's bootlegging. When my patrons serve it on a silver tray on Lake Shore Drive, it's hospitality."

A Miami police mug shot of a smiling Alphonse "Scarface Al" Capone. His popularity rivaled that of many celebrities of the era.

Capone in Charge

Al Capone's name is synonymous with crime and bootlegging in Chicago. He is the most infamous gangster of the era. Capone was the first gangster to enjoy true celebrity status. A master of public relations, he mingled with political, business, and social leaders and was well received by the general public, who actually cheered him when he went to the ballpark.

He demonstrated excellent leadership skills when handling men from rival gangs.

At the same time, he surrounded himself with gangsters he could trust. Capone appreciated what he called a hustler, in his eyes an honest crook. He considered himself nothing more than a hustler trying to make a living: "The men with power are the men with money or the will to take it. They break down into just two classes: the squares and the hustlers. I am a hustler, but I got respect for the squares." By squares, Capone meant Henry Ford or Thomas Edison, "a guy with brains and determination and a willingness to work for what he wants."[39]

His henchmen were very loyal, and Capone backed them to the limit. Unless he was double-crossed, Capone would do anything for his men. It is said that when sent off to do any dirty work for their boss, the men would chant, "All for Al, and Al for All!"[40]

Capone's base of operations was Chicago's Hawthorne Hotel, where his suite of rooms took up an entire floor. His office was lined with armor for protection from possible bullets or machine-gun fire. He also had a custom-built, armor-plated, seven-ton limousine.

By the time he was declared the FBI's Public Enemy Number One in 1927, Capone had amassed a fortune. He lived part-time in a twenty-five-room villa in

Al Capone conducted business from his armor-plated office in the Hawthorne Hotel. In 1927 alone, his criminal empire amassed a fortune of $105 million.

Florida and sported an 11.5-carat diamond ring. His cash take during that year from various rackets he ran in Chicago is listed as follows:

Beer, liquor, home brew	$60,000,000
Gambling places and dog tracks	$25,000,000
Brothels, dance halls	$10,000,000
Miscellaneous rackets	$10,000,000

Capone was wildly wealthy, but he was continually under threat of assassination from other gangsters. One by one, he eliminated his rivals. The blood flowed as Chicago became a lawless city.

Eliot Ness and the Untouchables

In 1928, Eliot Ness was put in charge of a special Prohibition detail set up specifically to go after Capone and his gang. Ness assembled a squad of nine agents who were dubbed "Untouchable"—in other words, unbribable. He searched hundreds of records to find men with spotless records who were also experts in various activities helpful in fighting bootleggers. Such skills included wiretapping, truck driving (for raids), and marksmanship.

Ness was supported by Prohibition agents, but he knew the Prohibition law was unpopular and upholding it would be difficult. "The trouble with the Prohibition law," he said, "was that such a large section of the public did not believe in it, either they were against it in its entirety or figured it was for the other fellow."[41]

The Chicago Prohibition Bureau employed three hundred agents. Capone's gangsters numbered one thousand. The odds were against Eliot Ness. But Ness threw himself into his work with a vengeance. The Untouchables raided many mob stills and distribution centers, costing Capone and his gang a considerable amount of money and garnering publicity from the press. Ness liked being in the public eye and always informed the press when a major raid was in the works.

Positive Press for Capone

The press also followed Capone's every move. Quite a showman, he knew the value of public goodwill. Free with his money, he often passed out large amounts

Eliot Ness (pictured) put together a squad of Untouchables (men with flawless records) to combat Capone and his legions of bootleggers.

to widows at funerals, left huge tips wherever he went, and threw money from his limousine to kids in the streets.

Capone also gave clothing to the poor and opened up a soup kitchen to feed the hungry of Chicago, endearing himself to the public. Press photographers captured his participation in these public services, careful to photograph only the right side of his face. "Scarface" Al Capone had received a jagged scar on the left side of his face during a knife fight in his youth and did not like the scar to show in pictures. Any photographer complying with his wishes received a fifty-dollar tip.

Capone was quick to point out that the soup kitchen cost $10,000 a month to operate. But he encouraged bakeries, coffee roasters, and meat packers to make contributions. Of course no one could safely refuse these charitable requests. Very little of Capone's money actually went to the soup kitchen. All the positive press was a calculated move designed to improve his popularity and provide a smokescreen for his bootlegging activities and other rackets.

Chicago Amnesia

Capone's empire grew to epic proportions. The corrupt police force was reluctant to become involved in the gang war problem. And when they did, prosecution of the gangsters was nearly impossible due to what became known as "Chicago Amnesia." Gangsters instilled such fear in possible witnesses that they quickly became reluctant to make positive identifications. Case after case was lost by the prosecution in court when witnesses suddenly refused

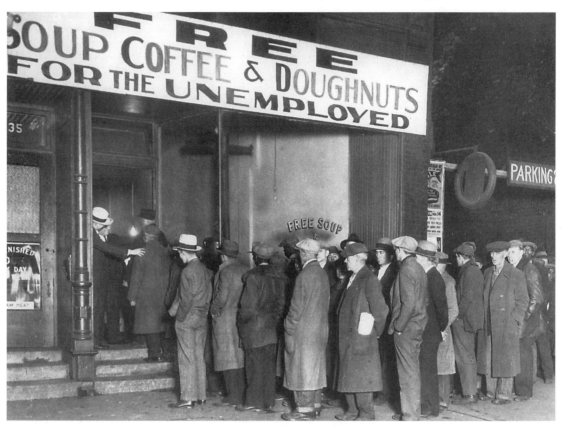

Though he was the FBI's Public Enemy Number One, Al Capone remained very popular with the people of Chicago. When he opened this soup kitchen to feed Chicago's hungry, his popularity grew even more.

to testify after a crime boss's order went out to his henchmen to "give them amnesia."[42] During the period of 1926–1927, the height of Capone's reign, no one was punished for any of the 130 gang murders that took place in Chicago. And the bloodiest gangland massacre was yet to come.

The St. Valentine's Day Massacre

The St. Valentine's Day massacre, the result of a protracted war between what was left of the old O'Banion gang and Capone, was planned to eliminate the current leader of the O'Banion gang, Bugs Moran. Moran ran the north side of town, a lucrative section, Capone wanted to take over. He arranged for Moran's gang to take delivery of a load of hijacked booze at the gang's headquarters, a garage on North Clark Street.

Capone oversaw the intricate planning of the operation by telephone from his Palm Island mansion in Florida. On the morning of February 14, 1929, several of Capone's henchmen, dressed in police uniforms, entered the garage and ordered

Seven members of Bugs Moran's gang were gunned down by Al Capone's rival gangsters in the St. Valentine's Day Massacre. One of the victims lived for three hours after the shooting but could not identify the gunmen.

the seven men inside against the wall. Believing it was a simple raid, the seven offered no resistance. The gangsters opened fire with machine guns, mowing down Moran's men. Then two of the gangsters put on overcoats and were escorted out with their hands in the air by the remaining "policemen." Witnesses believed it was a routine bust.

One of the victims lived for three hours after the shooting but could not identify the culprits. At first the killers were actually thought to be real police officers. Frederick Silloway, the local Prohibition administrator, told reporters that

the murderers were not gangsters. They were Chicago policemen. I believe the killing was the aftermath to the high-

jacking of 500 cases of whiskey belonging to the Moran gang by five policemen six weeks ago on Indianapolis Boulevard. I expect to have the names of these five policemen in a short time. It is my theory that in trying to recover the liquor the Moran gang threatened to expose the policemen and the massacre was to prevent exposure.[43]

Bugs Moran, Capone's main target, had overslept and was not at the garage that morning. When Moran was questioned during the ensuing investigation, he said, "Only Capone kills like that."[44]

Despite several eyewitnesses, physical evidence left at the garage, and offers of reward money, no one would ever be convicted of the killings. The public backlash against Capone, however, was dramatic. As a charitable bootlegger he was revered, but as a gangland assassin, the public turned on him, and the remaining members of Moran's gang vowed retaliation. Capone decided to lay low in a safe place. Upon returning from Florida, he arranged his own arrest on a gun charge and went to prison for a short time.

The authorities had never been able to keep Capone locked up on any serious charges. His final arrest, later in 1929, was for tax evasion.

Capone in Alcatraz

Capone was convicted and sent to a prison in Atlanta. In 1934, he was transferred to Alcatraz with prisoners considered to be the most dangerous in the penal system. He was assigned number eighty-five and was sent to work in the laundry, taunted by fellow prisoners and guards who enjoyed his humiliation. Later, he was assigned to cleaning the bathhouse. During his entire time in Alcatraz the most dignified duty he was allowed to perform was transferring books and magazines between the library and the cells.

A survivor of attempts on his life in prison, Capone was finally released in 1939 and returned to his mansion in Florida, where he spent his remaining days. Some of his old gang members visited him occasionally, but he was never again involved in any gang activity. He died in 1947.

As the seat of organized crime, Chicago suffered years of corruption and

Eliot Ness Stages a Raid

Eliot Ness related this story in his memoirs as quoted in Capone: The Man and the Era, *by Laurence Bergreen. The first major raid on a Capone brewery by Ness took place on the morning of March 11, 1931. It was carefully planned and ultimately successful but not without surprises for the agents involved.*

"I had a truck with a huge steel bumper on the front of it. No prisoners had ever been taken during a Capone brewery raid; it was our plan not to give them a chance to escape, so it was decided that we would drive the truck through the doors of the brewery; five of us riding in the truck and 10 in two other cars. . . . We put the truck into low gear, up the street and—*wham*—through the doors. The doors fell with a great loud clap, and at that moment my heart sank. There was no brewery! What I was looking at was a wooden wall, painted black, about two truck lengths' away from the front of the building, thus giving the illusion of a vacant garage. We soon found swinging doors in this wooden wall and were on the necks of five operators in less time than it took to tell it."

The St. Valentine's Day Massacre

Gang warfare reached a bloody climax on Valentine's Day in 1929 when seven men from the Bugs Moran gang were slaughtered by Capone's henchmen. A chilling account of that fateful morning is given in The Lawless Decade *by Paul Sann.*

"There were seven men in the garage at 2122 N. Clark Street, Chicago, on February 14, 1929—St. Valentine's Day. Five of them were in the Bugs Moran gang and they were waiting for the boss, who wanted a consignment of liquor convoyed from the Canadian border through the Prohibition force's paper curtain. . . .

But the black touring car that pulled up outside the garage at 10:30 that morning wasn't carrying the affluent Mr. Moran. It looked more like a police car. There was an alarm bell on the running board and a gun-rack behind the front seat. And out of it, moving briskly in the light snow and 18-degree cold, stepped two men dressed as policemen and two in civilian clothes. A fifth man in uniform stayed at the wheel. Inside the garage, the quartet whipped open their overcoats and produced two sawed-off shotguns and two machine guns. Somebody barked out an order—'Line-up! Put your noses to the wall!'—and then the artillery began to go off. The seven men standing against the red brick wall were cut down in a withering cross fire.

The four messengers of death left in a deceptive formation. The two in civies came out first, hands high, herded by the two in uniform as though they were under arrest. Sam Schneider, the tailor next door, heard the great clatter and saw the quartet depart; he thought the cops were simply taking in an errant pair trapped in gunplay in the cavernous booze drop. Witnesses in the rooming house across the street had the same idea."

terror at the hands of gangsters. It is estimated that gangsters pulled in more than $6 million weekly in their 1920s heyday. The cost to the citizens was more than $136 million per year in law enforcement, property damage, and the ineffectual court system. During Prohibition, nearly eight hundred gangsters were killed in mob warfare. Chicago's recovery from corrupt law officials and dirty politicians was slow and incomplete. Organized crime continued to thrive for decades.

5 President Harding and the Ohio Gang

While political corruption in the nation's cities was becoming more and more evident at the beginning of Prohibition, the election of Warren G. Harding as president in 1920 brought corruption all the way to the White House. Harding's administration was plagued with scandal from the beginning. Harding served as president from 1920 to 1923, when his unexpected death came just as news of various scandals was beginning to break.

Harding had promised the country a "return to normalcy" he was not able to deliver. A generous and friendly man, he seemed a good, steady candidate during a period of upheaval. He campaigned from the front porch of his home in Marion, Ohio, where thousands flocked to hear his soothing speeches:

> America's present need is not heroics, but healing; not nostrums, but normalcy; not revolution, but restoration; not agitation, but adjustment; not surgery, but serenity; not the dramatic, but the dispassionate; not experiment, but equipoise; not submergence in internationality, but sustainment in triumphant nationality.[45]

He was adept at flowery oration that consistently avoided addressing actual issues.

The Ohio Gang

When Harding came to Washington, he brought an entourage of friends and political cronies. Harding craved companionship and popularity, and he believed in loyalty. Misplaced loyalty would later prove to be his downfall.

Harding's friends, known as the Ohio Gang, set up headquarters in a small house at 1625 K Street. There, unknown to Harding, they dealt in liquor permits, pardons and paroles, and other illegal favors. Drinks were served to senators and congressmen, and cabinet members attended parties or stopped by to request favors. Actual bootlegging operations were even conducted from the premises with deliveries of liquor accepted in broad daylight.

It was relatively easy for the Ohio Gang to keep the president in the dark about their dirty dealings. Harding was a man more inclined to pacify than to stir up trouble, and he trusted his friends. He enjoyed the social aspects of being a politician much more than dealing with actual issues. He found his new position to be a difficult one and was often bewildered by the magnitude of his duties.

Harding was elected by the largest popular majority in American history to that point, 60.2 percent. He found himself in the White House facing a job he was ill equipped to handle. Harding was quickly overwhelmed. He admitted to a newspaper columnist: "Oftentimes, as I sit here, I don't seem to grasp that I am President!"[46]

He sought relief from the strain of the presidency through weekly poker meetings with his cronies. He also gave private parties upstairs in the White House, where only the best liquor was served. As president he was showered with gifts of liquor he was happy to share. Alice Roosevelt Longworth, daughter of former president Teddy Roosevelt, was once present at a party and was appalled at what she found:

When President Warren G. Harding brought his friends (known as the Ohio Gang) to Washington, they brought a plague of corruption and scandal with them.

"the air heavy with tobacco smoke, trays with bottles containing every imaginable brand of whisky stood about."[47]

Publicly, Harding declared he supported Prohibition. Privately, he continued to enjoy drinking as he always had with a certain degree of discretion. Downstairs at the White House, guests were served only lemonade and soft drinks. Harding appeared to be following the rules.

Harding Tries His Best

The president was a hard worker and put in many hours at his desk. His personal habit of avoiding conflict at all costs did not make him a strong leader. Hard work did not make up for a weak administration. And the Ohio Gang, by browbeating Harding, had secured important positions that enabled them to engage in their illicit activities quite easily.

Campaign manager Harry Daugherty, after finally achieving his goal of reaching Washington, was appointed attorney general by Harding. Together with Jess Smith, who held no official position but was known around town as the man to see to get things done, Daugherty collected millions of dollars from criminals buying immunity from prosecution of Prohibition laws. The attorney general's office became known as the Department of Easy Virtue.

Daugherty laundered the money earned by depositing it in a small bank in Ohio owned by Smith's brother. Investigation of this particular racket did not occur until 1924, after the president's death and after bank records had all been destroyed. Jess Smith, knowing the investigation was forthcoming and fearing indictment, had

A Friend to All

Warren G. Harding was a popular man. His philosophy on friendship and compromise gained him many admirers but also led to a multitude of scandals that plagued his presidency. His generous and flawed personality is examined in Robert K. Murray's The Politics of Normalcy.

Harding, though a popular and generous man, chose his friends poorly. He headed one of the most corrupt administrations in American history.

"Harding was perhaps best known for his friendliness and generosity. These two traits were extensions of his gregarious nature and also reflected his dislike of disharmony and contention. In both his private and his public life, he regarded compromise and conciliation as superior to argument and disagreement. Disagreement forestalled the resolution to problems while compromise enhanced it. Likewise, argument prevented the making of friends while conciliation aided it. Harding had a compulsive need for friends. . . .

Loyalty also was an extremely important element in the Harding personality. An acquaintance once remarked: 'He liked politicians for the reason that he loved dogs, because they were usually loyal to their friends.' To Harding, loyalty was not only a requirement for political self-preservation but necessary for a full and meaningful life. Unfortunately, under its mandate he too easily overlooked moral defects and was often indiscriminate in his personal contacts. While his fear of offending anyone, especially his friends, prompted him to grant their requests too readily, his emphasis on loyalty caused him to stand by them regardless of what they had done."

committed suicide in December 1923. Daugherty escaped jail as a result of two hung juries and his refusal to take the stand lest he incriminate himself.

It is likely that the president had become aware of his friends' illegal activities and that the stress of that knowledge contributed to his health problems shortly before his death. Daugherty maintained his innocence for the remainder of his life.

Another old poker-playing friend of Harding's, Charlie Forbes, was appointed head of the Veterans Bureau. He immediately became part of city nightlife. Forbes threw lavish parties outshining nearly everyone else's in the Washington social

Harry Daugherty (left), attorney general under Harding, avoided conviction for his part in turning the attorney general's office into what was known as the "Office of Easy Virtue."

scene. How he managed to do this on his meager salary of $10,000 a year was not questioned. Nor was his position at the Veterans Bureau monitored. Forbes took advantage of that fact.

The Veterans Bureau operated on a half-billion-dollar annual budget, and Forbes set to work in various underhanded dealings to increase the appropriation and to pocket much of that increase himself. He went on a transcontinental tour to select hospital sites with Elias Mortimer, a wealthy construction company executive. Forbes officially approved locations awarding building contracts to Mortimer's firm, which in turn gave Forbes huge kickbacks. For every new hospital, Forbes received a cash payment of at least $50,000.

Forbes also paid inflated prices for the land with bureau funds and split the difference with the sellers. In another sideline business, Forbes sold hospital equipment

at token prices for kickbacks from the buyers. He then replaced the stock, again using bureau money, at inflated prices and took a cut for every purchase. He squandered more than $33 million through his schemes and lavish lifestyle.

The president was enraged to learn of his friend's practices but protected him from the law by sending him overseas on a makeshift mission until the scandal cooled. After Harding's death, Forbes was sentenced to two years in prison with a $10,000 fine.

The Teapot Dome Scandal

By far the most serious and damaging blow to the Harding administration was the Teapot Dome scandal, masterminded by Albert Fall. Fall, another of Harding's cronies, had secured a cabinet appointment as secretary of the interior. Fall wanted to gain control of valuable oil-rich properties that were under navy jurisdiction. He solicited his friend, Secretary of the Navy Edwin Denby, to transfer the property over to Interior. Denby agreed over the objections of high-ranking naval officers. Harding, of course, stood by Fall. "I guess there will be hell to pay," he confided to a friend, "but those fellows seem to know what they're doing."[48]

Two of the most valuable naval oil reserve properties were Elk Hills in California and Teapot Dome in Wyoming. Fall secretly leased Elk Hills to his friend Edward Doheny, president of the Pan-American Oil Company, and Teapot Dome to Harry Sinclair, head of the Sinclair Consolidated Oil Corporation.

Doheny's lease required him to build a pipeline, a refinery in California, and oil storage tanks at Pearl Harbor. Sinclair was to build storage tanks and a pipeline for

Albert Fall, secretary of the interior, was convicted of taking bribes in the Teapot Dome scandal. He was sentenced to one year in jail and a fine of $100,000, which he never paid.

White House Parties

Lavish parties were held in secret at the White House during Prohibition. In Prohibition: Thirteen Years That Changed America *by Edward Behr, Alice Roosevelt Longworth, daughter of Theodore Roosevelt, shares her observations of what transpired.*

"No rumor could have exceeded the reality: the study was filled with cronies (Daugherty, Jess Smith), the air heavy with tobacco smoke, trays with bottles containing every imaginable brand of whiskey stood about, cards and poker chips ready at hand, an atmosphere of waistcoat unbuttoned, feet on desk, and spittoon alongside.

Harding [she added] was not a bad man. He was just a slob."

the navy, and to pay the government a royalty of 16 percent for twenty years. Even after these expenditures, both companies would rake in big profits.

Conservationists concerned over possible misuse of the land began an examination of Fall and his department. Fall resigned in 1923. After Harding's death, when knowledge of other scandals surfaced, an investigation was opened in earnest. Fall insisted he had never approached either Doheny or Sinclair for money in exchange for securing the leases. However, in January 1924, Doheny came forward and admitted he loaned Fall $100,000, but he insisted it had nothing to do with the leases. In the end, it was determined that Fall had also received $300,000 from Sinclair. Neither Doheny nor Sinclair was convicted of bribery, although Fall was convicted of taking bribes

and served nine months of a one-year jail term. His sentence also included a $100,000 fine, which he never paid.

Harding died ignorant of the Teapot Dome scandal and the damage it would do to his own reputation and the reputation of his administration. Considering his inaction in dealing with any hint of scandal, it is probable he would not have been able to respond to it effectively.

The President's Final Months

Harding's last days were not happy ones. By the autumn of 1922, he was physically exhausted. "I never find myself done," he lamented. "It seems as though I have been President for twenty years."[49]

Edward Doheny (second from right) testifies before the Senate committee investigating the Teapot Dome scandal. He was never convicted.

Harding felt overwhelmed by the responsibilities of the presidency and was distressed by his administration's scandals. During a cross-country tour in 1923, he suffered two heart attacks and died on August 2.

Mrs. Harding was also critically ill. Harding felt alone and abandoned. On top of his personal worries, news of White House scandals involving his cronies was beginning to reach him. Harding did not know whether to go public and launch an investigation or to try to cover up any problems that arose. Instead of dealing with the political problems at hand, Harding began a period of personal reform. Having long been criticized for his drinking habits, especially during Prohibition, Harding ceased having the White House poker parties and declared he was off liquor.

By the spring of 1923, his reelection campaign was in the planning stages. Harding was scheduled to deliver a series of speeches during a long cross-country train excursion to Alaska. He felt unwell but knew the speeches were crucial. He wanted to impress the voters and counter any damage rumors of scandal may have caused.

He addressed the issue of Prohibition for the final time during a speech in Denver, Colorado. The president was still refraining from drinking, determined to recover his health and his reputation:

The issue is fast coming to be recognized, not as one between wets and drys, not as a question between those who believe in prohibition and those who do not, not as a contention between those who want to drink and those who do not—it is fast being raised above all that—but as one involving the great question whether the laws of this country can and will be enforced.[50]

Harding Collapses

On July 26, after a speech in Seattle during the trip home, Harding collapsed in the extreme heat. He was helped back onto the train and continued on his way to the next stop, San Francisco. His personal physician diagnosed his problem as indigestion. Other physicians on board the train feared heart problems and arranged for a heart specialist to meet the president in San Francisco.

He was diagnosed as having coronary thrombosis. A blood clot was blocking the flow of blood to the president's heart. The seriousness of his condition was not revealed to Harding, who was simply ordered to rest.

At the Palace Hotel, on the evening of July 29, Harding survived another attack. By this time, the nation was aware of Harding's health problems. The newspapers reported the good news, but maintained a vigil outside the hotel.

On Thursday, August 2, 1923, the president was sitting with Mrs. Harding when he was seized with a convulsion and died. Mrs. Harding refused to allow an autopsy, but doctors believed the wandering blood clot had struck the president's brain. The nation was plunged into deep mourning. Harding, although an ineffectual president, was much loved.

Even as the bereaved nation buried the president, the scandals of the Harding administration were under investigation. Calvin Coolidge, who had served as vice president under Harding, was sworn in as president.

Coolidge as President

Coolidge was Harding's exact opposite in many ways. Harding had loved to socialize and entertain. Coolidge was so quiet he

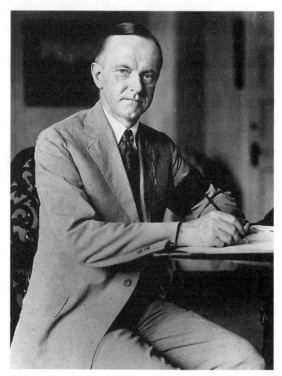

Though many thought him to be Harding's exact opposite, Calvin Coolidge (pictured) was an ineffective politician who did little to repair the damage that scandal had wreaked on the Harding administration.

earned the nickname "Silent Cal." He was a teetotaler who rarely went to parties. The Republicans hoped Coolidge would restore order to the White House and offer a sense of stability to the nation, which was reeling under the scandals that were being revealed.

Their hopes went unrealized. Although Coolidge was personally unlike Harding, politically he was also a weak leader and made few changes. He actually retained most of Harding's cabinet members, even Harry Daugherty.

Coolidge also did nothing to help Prohibition other than to set a good personal example. He did as little as possible as president, working only about four hours per day. A master of avoidance, Coolidge once remarked, "Never go out to meet trouble. If you will just sit still, nine times out of ten someone will intercept it before it reaches you."[51]

The Scandals Will Not Die

But the White House could not successfully ignore the Harding scandals, which haunted it for years. Even after the investigations and court cases were concluded, Nan Britton caused further scandal when she published her memoirs, *The President's Daughter*, in 1927, revealing details of her affair with Harding and about the daughter she bore him.

Harding had once commented, "I cannot hope to be one of the great presidents, but perhaps I may be remembered as one of the best loved."[52] The scandals that plagued him, even after his death, denied him that dream.

In June 1931, President Herbert Hoover eulogized Harding at a meeting of the Harding Memorial Association. His poignant words describe the tragedy of Harding and his administration:

Harding had a dim realization that he had been betrayed by a few of the men whom he had believed were his devoted friends. It was later proved in the courts of the land that these men had betrayed not only the friendship of their staunch and loyal friend but that they had betrayed their country.[53]

6 The Country in Turmoil

Mabel Willebrandt, deputy attorney general in charge of Prohibition enforcement for eight years, published a book after resigning her post in 1928. In *The Inside of Prohibition* she wrote, "No political, economic, or moral issue has so engrossed and divided all the people of America as the Prohibition problem, except the issue of slavery."[54] Willebrandt did not overstate Prohibition's impact on the country.

Prohibition had ushered in a period of flagrant disregard of the law, unprecedented crime, political and moral corruption, and division among the nation's citizens. The longer Prohibition remained in effect, the more evident its failure became. The public, disgusted with the entire matter, began to view it as a bad joke.

Will Rogers, the famous American humorist, proclaimed, "Prohibition is better than no liquor at all."[55] His humor reflected an obvious truth; liquor was available and finding it was only a small inconvenience.

The New York *Telegram* once assigned a team of reporters to investigate the availability of liquor in the borough of Manhattan. They managed to buy it in

dancing academies, drugstores, delicatessens, cigar stores, confectioners, soda fountains, behind partitions of shoeshine parlors, back rooms of barbershops, from hotel bellhops, from hotel headwaiters, night clerks, in express offices, in motorcycle delivery agencies, paint stores, malt shops, cider stubes, fruit stands, vegetable markets,

Although liquor was illegal, it was sold everywhere from clubs like New York's Maison Royal (pictured) to dancing academies and laundromats.

An Echo from the Past

With mounting evidence of failure, Prohibition stirred deep resentment and anger in the public chafing under its rule. Many who were previously dry started to question their allegiance. It is interesting to note Abraham Lincoln's views on the subject, voiced nearly one hundred years earlier as quoted in New Statesman *magazine, July 18, 1997.*

"Almost a century before Congress passed the 18th amendment to the Constitution of the United States, prohibiting the sale, manufacture and transportation of liquor, Abraham Lincoln warned that 'prohibition will work great injury to the cause of temperance. It is a species of intemperance within itself, for it goes beyond the bounds of reason in that it attempts to control a man's appetite by legislation, and makes a crime out of things that are not crimes.'"

Abraham Lincoln opposed Prohibition nearly 100 years before it became law.

---

groceries, smoke shops, athletic clubs, grill rooms, taverns, chophouses, importing firms, tearooms, moving-van companies, spaghetti houses, boarding houses, Republican clubs, Democratic clubs, laundries, social clubs, newspapermen's associations.[56]

Variety, a magazine of the entertainment world, frequently published the fluctuating prices of liquor at local speakeasies.

New York police commissioner Grover A. Whalen explained the enormity of controlling the liquor problem: "All you need is two bottles and a room and you have a speakeasy."[57]

Private citizens were indeed buying, making, and selling liquor. In fact, home brewing grew to immense proportions by the end of the twenties. The simple supplies needed were openly for sale in nearly every grocery store in the country. According to calculations based on the sale of hops, malt, and other ingredients (all legal purchases), the Prohibition Bureau estimated the quantity of beer brewed at home in 1929 alone to be almost 700 million gallons. Home wine makers spent about $220 million per year on wine presses, fermenting tubes, crocks, kegs, bottles, and corks to make wine from backyard vineyards.

The nation's thirst for liquor kept illegal stills like this one in business. Despite the fact that the homemade alcohol was often poisonous, people continued to drink it.

Prohibition was costing the average citizen on all fronts. Billions of dollars were spent to either make or buy liquor or to enforce Prohibition laws, and not one penny of tax revenue was being pumped back into the system. The rich could well afford to drink, but the poor were reduced to drinking bad home brew or dangerous rotgut. They were also easy prey for enterprising gangsters.

In Chicago, the Genna brothers set up a bootlegging racket in the poor section of town known as Little Italy. These mobsters hired hundreds of immigrant slum dwellers as so-called alky cookers for fif-teen dollars a day, installing stills in their kitchens and supplying them with the ingredients and operating directions. Alky cookers were common in the city slums, churning out hundreds of gallons of alcohol of varying degrees of quality. It all sold. Some of it was even safe to drink. Much of it was poisonous, but customers bought at their own risk.

The tragedy that occurred in the Bowery section of New York City was the most conclusive evidence of the toll poison alcohol was having on the poor. Bars in the Bowery and on the Lower East Side did not hesitate to serve wood alcohol and other poisonous concoctions when better stock was unavailable. "Bowery bums," desperate for alcohol and too poor to go elsewhere, drank whatever was available. During 1928, poison alcohol killed more than seven hundred people in the Bowery alone. There were similar instances of death by alcohol poisoning all over the country.

Wheeler Under Attack

Wayne Wheeler, leader of the Anti-Saloon League, came under attack for these deaths.

Although he denied any liability, it was the Anti-Saloon League that had sanctioned the continued manufacture and use of methyl alcohol throughout Prohibition. Methyl alcohol was known to be lethal, but the ASL lobbied against mandatory poison labels to be put on the bottles. They did not feel the labels were necessary, as methyl alcohol was not meant for consumption. Cartoons and newspaper editorials portrayed Wheeler as a cold-blooded poisoner.

Wheeler's response was inept at best. At first he denied that the poisonings ever happened. Then, when ridiculed by experts, he issued a press release declaring

Propaganda Under Attack

Clarence Darrow, in his book Prohibition Mania, *disputes popular propaganda of the times and makes light of conflicting theories while making a strong point. He refused to believe in charts, diagrams, or statistics, depending on his own reason to make up his mind on the issue. Like many, he believed Prohibition was not working.*

"Had the confident predictions of prohibitionists been fulfilled in the last 6 or 7 years, the United States to-day would be a veritable Utopia so far as crime, the social evil and consumption of narcotics are concerned. But, as everybody knows, those predictions have been falsified in every direction and in every particular, and if any improvement has taken place in the mental or physical health of the nation, such improvement is due to prosperity on the one hand, and, on the other, to ever increasing attention to and appropriations for the promotion of public health.

We are told, for example, by the health authorities of Chicago and Illinois that Chicago is the healthiest large city in the world to-day. Yet Chicago is notoriously one of the wettest cities in the country, and it would be far more logical to assert that the excellent health enjoyed by Chicago is attributable to drink than that the improvement in mental and physical health throughout the United States is due mainly to prohibition."

"the government is under no obligation to furnish people with alcohol that is drinkable when the Constitution prohibits it. The person who drinks this industrial alcohol is a deliberate suicide."[58] Through such callous comments, Wheeler greatly jeopardized his power and influence in political circles.

Homicide Rates on the Rise

Poisonous alcohol was not the only killer spawned by Prohibition. Homicide rates from gang wars were on the rise and were being publicized. The homicide rate climbed to 10 per 100,000 population during the 1920s, a 75 percent increase from the pre-Prohibition period.

Chicago had not cornered the market on bloody gangland-style killing. "Lucky" Luciano, a powerful gang leader in New York, was responsible for many murders. Luciano claimed he controlled every New York City police precinct through payoffs and that Police Commissioner Grover Whalen answered to him. Luciano sent Whalen $20,000 a month in banknotes as a form of friendly blackmail. Luciano also claimed he had given Whalen $35,000 to cover his margin after the stock market crash of 1929.

Whalen had, at one time, sent so many policemen out to raid speakeasies they became known as "Whalen's Whackers." As public opposition to Prohibition grew, and possibly as Whalen came more and more under Luciano's influence, Whalen had a change of heart and refused to send his officers out on raids. He claimed the cost to taxpayers was too great. Whatever his true reasons, this made Whalen the most popular man in town. Federal agents were left to handle enforcement on their own.

Wayne Wheeler's Woes

Denatured industrial alcohol was legal and tax exempt under provisions made in the Volstead Act, for which Wayne Wheeler, as author, was heavily criticized by the public. His predicament is examined in Prohibition by Edward Behr.

"So, for the first time, in early 1927, Wayne Wheeler, that master manipulator and moral scourge of godless drinkers, found himself on the defensive. Although he denied any liability, it was a fact that the ASL had originally sanctioned the use of methanol when the Volstead Act provisions were being drawn up, and had lobbied against any mandatory 'poison' labels on denatured alcohol. Wheeler had boasted of the ASL's key role in drafting the act so loudly, and so frequently, that he lacked all credibility now that he denied responsibility for some of its provisions."

New York police commissioner Grover Whalen (pictured) grew reluctant to send his officers out to raid speakeasies, partly due to pressure from gangster Lucky Luciano.

A Training Ground for Crooks

Federal enforcement agencies faced the tremendous problem of corrupt and inefficient Prohibition agents. The agents were so poorly paid, they often supplemented their income with payoffs from the criminals they were hired to arrest. Also because of the low pay scale, inexperienced men and men with criminal records of their own were the only ones to apply for the jobs.

Switching from enforcement to crime was not uncommon. "The Prohibition Service," said New Jersey's administrator, has proved to be a training ground for bootleggers. While in service, the agents, inspectors, and investigators naturally learn all the ropes of the underworld, as well as the government's methods in attempting to apprehend and convict violators. Naturally, when leaving the service of the prohibition forces, they are sought after by those engaged in illicit business.[59]

Another major concern and source of problems for the Prohibition Bureau was the number of deaths attributed to their agents. During the 1920s, the bureau admitted its agents killed 137 persons. The Customs Service and Coast Guard were responsible for another 36 deaths. Fifty-one killings were found to have been omitted from official Customs Service and Coast Guard reports. It was estimated that if killings by state and municipal officers had been included the number would have risen to more than 1,000.

During the same period of time, fifty-five Prohibition agents lost their lives in the line of duty, as well as fifteen Customs and Immigration officers and five enlisted Coast Guardsmen.

The Patriot's Prayer

Again, the newspapers fanned the controversy through cartoons, editorials, and sneering poetry that reflected the public's widespread disgust over the situation. One of the most popular poems of the day was "The Patriot's Prayer" by Arthur Lippman:

Now I lay me down to sleep—
My life and limb may Hoover keep,
And may no coast guard cutter shell

Prohibition agents Izzy Einstein and Moe Smith with a still they captured in a New York City basement. By 1929, local authorities had left enforcement of Prohibition up to the federal government.

This little home I love so well.
May no dry agent shooting wild
Molest mine wife and infant child.
Or, searching out some secret still,
Bombard my home to maim and kill.
When dawn succeeds the gleaming stars,
May we, devoid of wounds and scars,
Give thanks we didn't fall before
The shots in Prohibition's War.[60]

Bowing to public opinion, city and state police forces all over the country quietly began an enforcement retreat, taking New York City's lead and leaving it up to federal agents. President Harding had once issued the warning that "if any state dragged its feet, the Feds would be compelled to enter its territory and jurisdiction to set up the necessary police and judicial functions, whereupon the most difficult and trying situations would inevitably arise."[61] In actuality, it was not a warning but rather exactly what the states hoped would happen. As the decade wore on, state and local police did less and less, helping federal agents only when necessary.

President Hoover Gets Tough

President Herbert Hoover had a much stronger approach. During his administration (1929–1933) he increased funds earmarked for enforcement and demanded action. The cost to the taxpayers was high. The annual budget of the Prohibition Bureau, which had started at a mere $4.4 million, rose to $13.4 million. Coast Guard spending added another $13 million per year to that figure.

Yet Hoover's decisive attitude worked —too well. Prohibition agents previously

President Herbert Hoover more than tripled the budget for Prohibition enforcement in a successful effort to crack down on bootleggers.

concerned only with gangsters, bootleggers, and speakeasies began arresting average citizens for minor infractions of the Prohibition laws. Americans were outraged. The vast majority did not feel the "innocent" man on the street should be harassed for laws he did not support. The conflict over Prohibition grew as more and more arrests were made.

The Crowded Court System

Convictions for liquor offenses in federal courts rose from an average of 35,000 in 1922 to 61,383 by 1932. The court system was bogged down with cases too numerous to handle.

In New York City during the peak crime year of 1926 it was estimated that if all violators of the Volstead Act during a single month (four hundred to five hundred cases) demanded a jury trial, every federal judge available for Prohibition cases would be occupied for a year. To avoid having the entire court system grind to a halt, "bargain days" were set aside to handle the overflow. On these days pending cases were disposed of without a jury by promising defendants light sentences if they would plead guilty.

Hoover's strenuous efforts for justice at the end of the decade only made matters worse.

Federal Prisons Packed Beyond Their Capacity

The federal prisons were overflowing with prisoners. In 1920 the number of prisoners serving long-term sentences was 5,000. By 1930, this number had risen to 12,000 with more than 4,000 of those convicted serving time for violating liquor laws. Existing federal prison capacity was only 7,000. Prisons such as Atlanta Penitentiary and Leavenworth in Kansas were designed to house 1,500 prisoners each; by the end of the decade, each prison held more than 3,700 men.

It was during this time that Alcatraz and five more federal prisons were approved for construction. Again, the tremendous cost fell on the taxpayers. Federal expenditures in the penal system rose more than 1,000 percent from pre-Prohibition times. The angry public, wanting repeal, began pressuring Washington.

Corruption in the Capital

Washington, D.C., was experiencing many problems as a result of Prohibition. Political conflicts were numerous, and the crime rate had skyrocketed as much as, if not more than, that of many other major cities. Arrests for drunkenness totaled 3,565 at the beginning of Prohibition. Five years later, the total was 9,149 and climbing.

Drunken activity was evident even in the Capitol Building. A sign on the door of one small, inconspicuous room containing a few chairs, an empty desk, and book-lined shelves said "Board of Education." The various politicians and others who visited this room simply referred to it as "the library." In reality, it was a drinking parlor. The books concealed an abundance of liquor. Legislators would stop in during working hours for refreshment. Capitol workers and legislators saw many senators and representatives emerge from the "library" in a drunken condition. Some even voted on the passage of bills while drunk, though the public rarely heard about such behavior.

The Federal Building was another source of problems. More than fifty thousand violators were arraigned there every year. Many deals were struck and payoffs made inside its walls. One bootlegger even scattered handbills advertising his liquor prices in an effort to drum up business. Corruption permeated the entire building.

Emory S. Buckner, U.S. attorney for the southern district of New York, described his experience in the Federal Building before a Senate subcommittee:

Emory S. Buckner, U.S. attorney for the southern district of New York, was disgusted with the amount of corruption he saw in the Federal Building in Washington, D.C.

Fifty thousand protesters march in an anti-Prohibition parade in New York. Though it remained law for 13 years, the Volstead Act was extremely unpopular with a large segment of the population.

I found the fifth floor of the Federal Building a seething mob of bartenders, peddlers, waiters, bond runners, fixers. . . . Federal judges have told me . . . that the whole atmosphere of the Federal Building was one of pollution, that the air of corruption had even descended into the civil parts of the court, and reports were made . . . of attempts to bribe jurymen even in the toilets of the building.[62]

The Tide Turns

Even diehard Prohibitionists began to realize they were losing ground. Years of corruption and controversy had turned the tide against them. Repeal was no longer an empty threat or idle wish. Influential people were beginning to speak out in its favor. The only thing that could save Prohibition was the number of votes necessary to make repeal an actuality. No amendment to the Constitution had ever been repealed, and many thought it would simply never happen.

Clarence Darrow, the famous defense attorney, was personally opposed to Prohibition but still doubted it would ever be repealed. "Thirteen dry states with a population less than that of New York State alone can prevent repeal until Halley's Comet returns," he reasoned. "One might as well talk about taking his summer vacation on Mars."[63]

Senator James A. Reed of Missouri, during a Prohibition debate in 1928, denounced the drys for failing in their purpose:

The bar is condensed into a gripsack. The sales are by the case instead of by the glass. The saloon is still here, and more people are engaged in the business than in pre-Volstead days. You did not exterminate the brewery, you made millions of little breweries and installed them in the homes of people.[64]

Politicians, especially in the northern states, found they had to support a wet platform to be elected. Wet pressure groups abounded. The drys tried to say these groups were secretly financed by the liquor trade. In truth, the people were speaking out against an unpopular law that had caused nothing but problems from its inception.

Drys then tried to mollify the wet pressure groups by suggesting the Volstead Act be modified, not repealed. The wets did not believe modification would work. Industrialist John D. Rockefeller Jr. was against modification and expressed his views in a letter to repeal supporter Dr. Nicholas Murray Butler. Rockefeller's support for repeal greatly helped the cause:

When the Eighteenth Amendment was passed I earnestly hoped . . . that it would be generally supported by public opinion and thus the day be hastened when the value to society of men with minds and bodies free from the undermining effects of alcohol would be generally realized. That this has not been the result, but rather that drinking has generally increased; that the speakeasy

has replaced the saloon . . . that a vast army of lawbreakers has been recruited and financed on a colossal scale; that many of our best citizens . . . have openly and unabashedly disregarded the Eighteenth Amendment; that as an inevitable result respect for all law has been greatly lessened; that crime has increased to an unprecedented degree —I have slowly and reluctantly come to believe. . . .

In my judgment it will be so difficult for our people as a whole to agree in advance on what the substitute (for the Eighteenth Amendment) should be, and so unlikely that any one method will fit the entire nation, that repeal will be far less possible if coupled with an alternative measure. For that reason I the more strongly approve the simple, clear-cut position you are proposing to recommend and which I shall count it not only a duty but a privilege to support.[65]

Prohibition and the Depression

The stock market crash of 1929 sent the nation spinning into a major depression. Wet propagandists accused Prohibition of contributing to the depression. Their reasons were based on fact. While it is impossible to predict what would have happened if the stock market crash had not occurred, Prohibition had undermined and weakened the nation's economy.

The destruction of the brewing and distilling industry put more than a million men out of work. Farmers lost millions in income when brewing operations were halted by the Volstead Act. With grain supplies such as hops and barley no longer in demand by the brewing industry an agricultural depression resulted. The demand for hops and barley for home brewing use, although considerable, could not make up for the loss of legitimate avenues of sale for the farmer's products. The economy suffered in other ways, too. The large amount of government spending on enforcement depleted the nation's coffers. The huge loss of federal revenue caused by the elimination of the liquor tax hurt the economy even more.

The onset of the depression and the continuing propaganda spread by wet activists influenced the candidates' platforms and the voters' opinions in the presidential election of 1932. Though Prohibition took a backseat to the depression in debates on major issues, candidates were pressed to reveal where they stood on the issue of repeal.

A New President Is Elected

During a speech in St. Louis, Democrat Franklin D. Roosevelt indicated his support of repeal when he told the crowd he would "increase the federal revenue by several hundred million dollars a year by placing a tax on beer."[66]

The Republicans urged Hoover to support repeal as a matter of political strategy,

An October 24, 1929, newspaper headline announces the stock market crash. Many anti-Prohibitionists reasoned that the Volstead Act was responsible for the crash and America's subsequent plunge into the Great Depression.

but he refused to do so. The Constitution, as it stood after the Volstead Act, forbade alcohol and Hoover insisted that the presidential oath he had taken was "to preserve, protect and defend the Constitution." [67] His reservation, however noble, certainly was a factor in his losing the election.

Nine days after taking office, Roosevelt sent a special message to Congress urging legalization of 3.2 percent beer.

Seven days later, a bill had been passed and was signed by the president redefining intoxicating liquor as being above 3.2 percent alcohol. As of April 7, 1933, real beer would once again be legal.

Beer Is Back

Outside the breweries German bands played as crowds gathered with noisemakers. More than fifteen thousand free bottles of beer were passed out by Pabst, Schlitz, and other breweries. The 331 breweries in the country began working overtime to fill the demand, many borrowing milk trucks to make deliveries.

The boost to the economy was immediate. Twelve million dollars' worth of trucks and $15 million worth of advertising were ordered by the breweries. A Los An-

March 26, 1933, marked the beginning of the end for Prohibition. Here, President Franklin D. Roosevelt, with members of Congress, signs a bill permitting the brewing of beer with an alcoholic content of 3.2 percent.

Even the evangelist Billy Sunday, who was one of Prohibition's staunchest supporters, realized that repeal of the Volstead Act was on the horizon.

geles brewery ordered 600,000 bottles. Another brewery ordered 80 million labels. Frigidaire jumped from a three-day work-week to a six-day workweek to fill orders for cooling equipment and larger home refrigerators that would accommodate beer bottles. Even the pretzel industry went into overtime production to fill demand. In three months' time, only tobacco and federal income tax produced more revenue for the nation than beer.

The drys were devastated, still stubbornly clinging to the belief that repeal would not happen, but the majority of people realized it was inevitable. Even Billy Sunday, the famous evangelist and a staunch supporter of Prohibition, threw in the towel. "I can't continue to preach Prohibition and preach the gospel," he said. "I'm not as strong as I used to be, and the load is too heavy. So, I'm returning to my first love—preaching the gospel." [68]

The nation celebrated; the end of Prohibition was surely on its way.

Chapter

7 Women and Repeal

The Women's Organization for National Prohibition Reform (WONPR), founded in 1929, was one of the strongest and most influential organizations of its time. Its impact on the repeal movement was profound. By the end of the twenties, it was evident that the majority of the public was anxious for repeal of the Eighteenth Amendment. The WONPR effort for repeal was both timely and effective. This group of upper-class women led a grassroots campaign that star-

tled politicians and pushed the repeal movement to a successful end. The WONPR was one of the last organizations formed during the turbulent Prohibition years. Many groups had been actively working for repeal for years. Their methods were studied by the WONPR and helped the women achieve their goals.

One powerful group, the Association Against the Prohibition Amendment (AAPA), was founded in 1918 and became

Members of the Women's Organization for National Prohibition Reform (WONPR) in Birmingham, Michigan, conduct a vigorous campaign against Prohibition in 1930.

Declaration of Principles of WONPR

The Women's Organization for National Prohibition Repeal spearheaded a huge and ultimately successful campaign to stop Prohibition. Its Declaration of Principles is listed in Grace Root's informative book Women and Repeal.

"1. We are convinced that National Prohibition is fundamentally wrong.

(a) Because it conflicts with the basic American principles of local home rule and destroys the balance, established by the framers of our government, between powers delegated to the Federal authority and those reserved to the sovereign states or to the people themselves,

(b) And because its attempt to impose total abstinence by national governmental fiat ignores the truth that no law will be respected or can be enforced unless supported by the moral sense and the common conscience of the communities affected by it.

2. We are convinced that National Prohibition, wrong in principle, has been equally disastrous in consequences in the hypocrisy, the corruption, and the tragic loss of life and the appalling increase of crime which have attended the abortive attempt to enforce it; in the checking of the steady growth of temperance which had preceded it; in the shocking effect it has had upon the youth of the nation; in the impairment of constitutional guarantees of individual rights; in the weakening of the sense of solidarity between the citizen and the government which is the only sure basis of a country's strength."

---

incorporated just a few months after the Volstead Act was ratified and before it actually took effect. As soon as ratification occurred, the AAPA announced its goals:

> This association has two immediate aims: (1) To prevent the country from going on a bone-dry basis on July 1, and (2) to make the Eighteenth Amendment forever inoperative.

> It daily prophesies failure, justifies violation of the law, opposes enforce-

ment, throws its influence on the side of lawlessness when it ought to be on the side of law and order.

> The leader in the whole movement to discredit the law and make it "inoperative" as originally promised by it, is the Association Against the Prohibition Amendment.[69]

The AAPA continued its fight throughout Prohibition, spearheaded by the group's many business and industrial

Business and industry groups threw their power and financial strength into the fight against Prohibition, garnering support for repeal from politicians and the public.

leaders. The 103 directors on its roster served on boards of businesses with more than 2 million employees and assets of $40 billion.

These powerful men distributed literature, books, and pamphlets urging repeal. They also pressured politicians to adopt wet platforms and policies. Their influence helped sway public opinion against Prohibition. By 1926 a Newspaper Enterprise Association poll conducted through 326 newspapers in all forty-eight states showed 81 percent of the people supported either modification or full repeal.

Newspapers and magazines consistently ran more pro-wet articles than dry. By 1931 a survey showed circulation of wet newspapers outnumbered dry newspapers 2 to 1. Organizations such as the AAPA and media endorsement for repeal led to major conflict by the end of the twenties.

Modification Splits Drys

Total repeal may not have happened if drys across the country had not been split in their allegiance. Many drys believed in modification, but diehard teetotalers would not support them in their modification efforts. Wets, hoping to mollify the situation, were willing to support modification. In fact, their slogan was Beer and Light Wines Now, but No Saloon Ever.[70] Staunch teetotalers rejected this notion, and the war for repeal intensified.

Business and industry leaders who supported repeal did not do so strictly out of concern for what was best for the country; self-interest was a major motivation. The government was losing an estimated half-billion dollars per year by not having a liquor tax. The rich were overburdened with taxes in an effort to compensate for this loss. Many believed repeal, and thus the ensuing liquor tax revenue, would lessen the burden on the rich and give them more money to invest in business and industry. Money invested would help the devastated economy. The time was ripe for a fresh repeal campaign when the WONPR was formed and began its mission.

Mrs. Sabin Speaks Out

The national chairman and founder of the WONPR was Mrs. Charles Sabin. Her husband was chairman of the board of the Guaranty Company of New York, a treasurer and a director of the Sutton Place South Corporation, chairman of the board of the Intercontinental Rubber Company, and a trustee of the Mackay Companies. He was also active in the AAPA. Pauline Sabin was also politically active. She was the first woman to serve on the National Republican Committee.

On April 3, 1929, at a lunch given in her honor, Mrs. Sabin announced she had resigned from her position at the National Republican Committee because she wanted to work for a change in the Prohibition law. She had been disillusioned by President Hoover and his lack of action in studying the failure of Prohibition and in advocating any changes. Mrs. Sabin's declaration caused an immediate and dramatic reaction:

> When I said . . . I was going to fight prohibition, the letters began pouring in from all over the country. . . . I found I had spoken for thousands of other women. There was a large group ready to be organized, wanting to be organized. . . . I could not turn back from it.[71]

The WONPR Is Formed

In less than two months, twenty-four women met in Chicago to launch the Women's Organization for National Prohibition Reform. These women were all society leaders with money and leisure time to devote to the organization. Their affluence was critical to the success of the WONPR. Many women wanted to become involved just to work with this elite group. To be one of "Sabin's Women" meant immediate social acceptance and prestige.

At the Chicago meeting Mrs. Sabin announced that 121 women representing twenty-six states had agreed to serve on a national committee that would become part of the group's permanent organizational plan. It was decided that there would be no membership dues; the

WONPR would be funded entirely by voluntary contributions. A convention was planned to take place that fall. Five national committees were established, with their tasks outlined as follows:

1. Investigation: to gather statistics regarding the increase of drunkenness and the effect of Prohibition on the younger generation; to get statements on Prohibition from judges of juvenile courts, social service workers, educators, etc.

2. Publicity: to write open letters to the newspapers and to answer statements found in the press from organizations supporting Prohibition.

3. Speakers' Bureau: to train women to speak at meetings, hearings, and conventions.

4. Legislative: to follow all legislation pertaining to Prohibition in federal and state legislatures and to be prepared to appear at legislative hearings as representatives of the Organization.

5. Membership: to enroll members throughout the forty-eight states.[72]

The Drys React

More than five hundred newspapers reported on the meeting and the aims of the newly formed organization. Sabin's Women had caused quite a stir. The drys were outraged. Dr. Mary Armor, known as "the Georgia Cyclone," president of the Woman's Christian Temperance Union in her state, declared, "As to Mrs. Sabin and her cocktail-

When the WONPR began to actively campaign for repeal, groups such as the Woman's Christian Temperance Union (shown here delivering their anti-alcohol message to bar patrons) reaffirmed their commitment to Prohibition.

Support for Repeal

The WONPR gained support rapidly and was recognized as a competent and powerful adversary of Prohibition. In the book Women and Repeal, *Alfred E. Smith of New York regards the WONPR movement as a turning point in the fight for repeal.*

"Sensible women who had been misled by the dry slogan that all good women must be for drastic enforcement of the Eighteenth Amendment began to realize that they were supporting a movement more dangerous to the home, more harmful to children, more threatening to future generations, than anything else in American life. When the ideas of the fanatics began to lose their hold upon the country, when courageous women like Mrs. Sabin risked public condemnation by attacking the whole theory of the Eighteenth Amendment, the Drys who had had everything their own way were put on the defensive. When women entered the fight for Repeal, sanity began to return to the country."

drinking women, we will out-live them, out-fight them, out-love them, out-talk them, out-pray them and out-vote them."[73]

The WONPR immediately began its campaign with unbridled enthusiasm and diligence. Its first step was to build a large and active organization in each state and to enlist new members. By the end of the first year membership grew from an initial 100,000 to 300,000 with organizations active in thirty-three states.

The Women Go Door to Door

Of all methods used to enlist new members, door-to-door canvasing was the most popular and effective. The women traveled from city to city, stopping at each house to chat with people and discuss

their platform in a friendly manner. The hardworking women were quite successful in bringing about a tolerant attitude toward repeal. Sometimes they were met with bold opposition, having doors slammed in their faces and having dogs set upon them to drive them away. In some cities the police refused to let the women make their rounds. Still, the women persisted with their campaign.

Each state was approached in a manner deemed to have the most chance of success pertaining to that state's individual needs. In Michigan many rural areas were known to be dry. The WONPR faced the opposition head-on, targeting these rural areas and enlisting members from them. In California, speakers addressed groups such as labor unions, laundry workers, and waitress unions. In New York, WONPR members made appearances at women's clubs, often with drys speaking at the same meeting. Racial groups were canvased by members of their own community. Booths were set up at state and county fairs across the country and women passed out literature and spoke to the public.

While housewives made up the majority of the membership (more than 50 percent) the balance comprised a diverse group of women, including teachers, nurses, secretaries, policewomen, astrologists, social workers, clerks, and manual workers. Women of all classes, occupations, and beliefs were being drawn together to fight against Prohibition.

The discovery of an article containing anti-Prohibition sentiments attributed to Confederate President Jefferson Davis greatly helped the repeal cause in the southern states.

WONPR Members in Training

The WONPR recognized the importance of training its members to be effective. Free classes were held on public speaking to help members prepare themselves to make public appearances. They were also trained in debate. WONPR members often debated the repeal issue on the radio with dry community leaders and spokespersons. Bilingual members of the WONPR were sent to speak to non-English-speaking groups and communities. No members were asked to do work they were unprepared for.

Publicity for the group was spread by radio, newspapers, public mass meetings, and through distribution of flyers and circulars. The women constantly searched out new ways of getting their platform to the public.

The Repeal Cause Gains Momentum

One dramatic triumph for the WONPR took place in Kentucky, a state that had been stubbornly dry. The Kentucky state secretary for the WONPR, Gense J. Brashear, discovered an old scrapbook in a secondhand shop that contained newspaper clippings dating from the 1860s. One article quoted Jefferson Davis, the Confederate president during the Civil War, stating his opposition to Prohibition. After the article was verified as authentic, the story was run on the front page of the Louisville *Courier Journal.* This greatly helped the cause for repeal throughout the southern states.

Nothing Left to Chance

The grueling schedule of activities WONPR members maintained for months before the crucial 1932 elections is described in Women and Repeal. *Typical of their overall dedication to the cause, the nonstop push for success forever changed the country's attitude toward women at the polls. The WONPR's determination to get women out to vote educated, inspired, and united women of all backgrounds.*

"Campaign headquarters were maintained in most of the states by the WONPR. In many places these were established in cooperation with the Association against the Prohibition Amendment or other Repeal groups. In Alabama the WONPR held the fort alone, and did it with brilliant success. For three months before the November election, weekly meetings were held, with speeches from labor representatives, doctors, lawyers, legionnaires, and such politicians as were willing to come out openly for Repeal. In New Hampshire the State Chairman, Mrs. Skinner, campaigned throughout the state with such determination that the WONPR was generally given credit for the subsequent victory at the polls. Connecticut gave demonstrations on [the use of] voting machines, posted sample ballots, held meetings and broadcasts, distributed publicity and flyers and in two counties secured permission to put literature in every R.F.D. box. In Philadelphia the WONPR 'shop' headquarters installed a voting machine for demonstration, and against the opposition of the local political powers, succeeded in securing the adoption of that method of voting. A special center was maintained for educational work among colored women.

Election Day was a day of gruelling hard work for thousands of WONPR officers and members. Motor contingents conveyed hordes of voters to the polls. Volunteer workers assisted at the polls, distributed Repeal buttons on the streets, climbed millions of steps and rang countless doorbells, rounding up the vote. Publicity campaigns wound up in a burst of oratory. Many a woman will remember the day of November 8, 1932, as the busiest day of her life."

The WONPR historian of Kentucky later wrote, "At a time when we needed help in breaking through the wall of prejudice in the South, there came the voice of the Southern Chieftain giving his views on individual liberty and moral responsibility. It was a timely discovery."[74]

The WONPR was not solely concerned with publicity and the education of its members. Statistics (many very damaging

One of "Sabin's Women" registers at a New York WONPR convention. The WONPR's political power was considerable, and it continued to grow throughout Prohibition.

to Prohibition) were gathered concerning various facets of the problem and a study examined the effects of Prohibition on blacks in the state of North Carolina. In Philadelphia, a report was compiled concerning the alarming number of court cases relating to violation of the Prohibition laws and of bad liquor. In Delaware, a committee was formed to research the conditions of liquor control in that state before and after Prohibition. WONPR members also polled members of Congress on their stand on repeal.

The political power of the WONPR grew rapidly. The WONPR publicly supported candidates known to be wet and denounced the drys. Politicians were increasingly wary of taking positions opposed by the organization. Newspapers continually covered WONPR activity. Failure to gain their endorsement, or worse,

being denounced by them was damaging to a political career. Sabin's Women were a force to be reckoned with.

The WONPR pressured politicians to take a stand on the repeal issue and to voice their opinions. During primary elections in Pennsylvania in 1930, politicians waffled on the issue or avoided it entirely. The WONPR organized its members and took action. The WONPR state historian for Pennsylvania recorded their efforts:

> Political headquarters were established wherever possible, in charge of volunteer workers in the drive to elect the Repeal candidates, Phillips, Dorrance and Bohlen. At the suggestion of Mrs. Lewis Laurence Smith, a survey of the State was made. Every county chairman was required to follow up each State and Federal candidate, and each

political office holder in her district, from Committeeman to Senator, to drive them out into the open and force them to stop straddling the Prohibition question.[75]

The WONPR operated on a state-by-state basis; the women gained experience that strengthened their self-assurance and political power. Valiant strides accomplished during the first two years of the WONPR's existence validated the group's influence. Their methods of publicity, research, education, and political action influenced every community in the country.

The Second National Conference

The Second National Conference of the WONPR was held in Washington, D.C., in April 1931. Five hundred delegates were expected, but more than eight hundred came. The conference, as reported by the press, was efficient, run with precision, and extremely busy. There were many meetings of different committees and state delegates. Delegates from thirty-three states were present. Because details had been expertly planned in advance, there was never a pause in the parliamentary proceedings.

Different plans of action and resolutions were offered by individual states. The resolution put forth by New York most reflected the goals and mission of the organization:

WHEREAS, in 1929 the WONPR was organized to record the dissatisfaction of the women of the United States with conditions resulting from the passage of the Eighteenth Amendment and the National Prohibition Act; and,

WHEREAS, in 1930 the WONPR, in order to overcome such conditions, undertook to work for the Repeal of the Eighteenth Amendment and return to each state of its power to regulate the manufacture, sale and transportation of intoxicating beverages; and,

WHEREAS, such repeal and return of power to each state requires action by Congress and the legislatures of the States; and,

WHEREAS, the Eighteenth Amendment and the National Prohibition Act, with their consequent abuses of wide-spread intemperance, hypocrisy and corruption, threaten the structure of our Government and create an issue so important as to transcend party affiliations,

BE IT RESOLVED, that it is in the sense of this Conference that in order to effect the Repeal of the Eighteenth Amendment, the WONPR urge its members to support only those candidates for public office who have openly declared themselves in favor of the Repeal of the Eighteenth Amendment.[76]

The resolution was unanimously approved and forwarded to the political activities committee.

More than five hundred WONPR delegates, led by Mrs. Sabin, were received at the White House the following morning. There they presented a petition stating the group's position against Prohibition. Their determination to make repeal an integral issue in the upcoming 1932 elections was noted by Washington papers. Leading politicians wanted to keep the issue in the background. Sabin's Women were not going to allow that to happen.

Letters Sent to Congress

The WONPR sent letters to each member of Congress urging them to submit the repeal issue for a vote, arguing that whether or not one was individually for or against repeal, the people of the country should be allowed to vote on the matter.

In December the results of the letter campaign were compiled. Two hundred and fifty-one replies had been received. More than half favored submitting the issue for public vote. WONPR activity toward this end intensified.

The total membership swelled to an astonishing 600,000 women, and chapters in all states convened strategy sessions to determine ways to arouse interest in the issue and to educate the public. The WONPR began to work actively with other anti-Prohibition groups. Mass meetings and public debates were held all over the country. In New Mexico, where a large portion of the population spoke only Spanish, preparations were made for a bilingual speaking tour. Publicity material was distributed in the foreign language press.

Delegates and members in each state made a concerted effort to muster voting strength. It was crucial that only candidates favoring repeal be voted into office. Members made personal contacts to verify candidates' and voters' opinions on the issue. They published results of questionnaires concerning repeal and pushed the repeal issue to the forefront in every political contest. Dry candidates began to lose

ground and many were forced from office during primary elections.

Again, the WONPR attacked Congress, sending telegrams to all members of Congress who had declared they were for submission of the repeal issue but had not yet signed the petition to have the resolution brought to the floor for discussion.

Presidential Candidates Questioned

In April 1932, telegrams were also sent to all eight presidential and vice-presidential candidates, asking,

Franklin D. Roosevelt replied favorably to the WONPR's 1932 poll of presidential candidates asking if they would support repeal of the Volstead Act.

Will you if nominated . . . support a plank in your party platform to submit the question of the Repeal of the Eighteenth Amendment and the return to each state of its former power to regulate the manufacture, sale and transportation of intoxicating beverages within its own limits to conventions held in the several states for ratification or rejection.[77]

Four favorable replies were received and were made public. Franklin D. Roosevelt replied favorably. No record of reply exists from President Hoover.

A Test of Honor

The presidential election was a test of solidarity for the members of the WONPR. Many of the women, including Mrs. Sabin, were staunch Republicans. But Roosevelt, a Democrat, was clearly the candidate to support concerning the repeal issue. President Hoover fully intended to continue to support Prohibition. Mrs. Sabin urged members to vote for Roosevelt. Though the president of the United States did not have the power to veto or change a proposed amendment, the prestige of the office would certainly influence legislation. Many women, used to voting a straight party ticket, were torn, but the WONPR, after much discussion, decided to remain loyal and unified and passed a resolution to endorse Roosevelt.

This resolution resulted in the resignation of 150 members, but 137,000 new members joined the organization in approval. Personal political affiliations were put aside for the good of the cause. The members rallied together and threw themselves into the task of garnering votes for Roosevelt and other wet candidates.

Election Day

The WONPR continued publicity campaigns, debates, and public meetings right up to election day. Their activities on election day itself were vigorous and well organized. The women drove voters to the polls, distributed repeal buttons on the streets, and rang hundreds of doorbells to round up the vote.

As the results came in, it was evident their campaign had succeeded even beyond their own hopeful expectations. In state after state, wet senators and representatives were being elected to office. Franklin Roosevelt won by a landslide in depression-weary and Prohibition-weary America.

Finishing the Job

The Fourth National Conference of the WONPR took place in Washington in April 1933. The focus was on ratification of a repeal amendment and regulation of a reinstituted liquor industry. The Twenty-first Amendment, which would repeal the Eighteenth Amendment, had passed both houses of Congress that February. The Eighteenth Amendment would be null and void once thirty-six states voted for ratification. The Twenty-first Amendment, which effectively abolished Prohibition, allowed individual states to regulate their own liquor laws. This was acceptable to the

WONPR, and the group resolved to concentrate on state ratifications. It was also decided that once ratification took place, the WONPR would take steps to disband.

As ratification was put to the vote state by state, the WONPR printed the actual ballots in newspapers with instructions on casting votes for ratification. Instructions were also printed in foreign-language papers. The WONPR launched a nonstop radio campaign urging the public to get out and vote. Door-to-door canvasing continued by volunteer workers and WONPR members. And state by state, the battle was won.

Prohibition Ends

On December 5, 1933, the necessary thirty-sixth state ratified the amendment. Roosevelt signed the proclamation ending Prohibition at 7:00 P.M. The chairman of the New York State Alcohol Control Board, Edward P. Mulrooney, stayed at his desk all night validating one thousand licenses for speakeasies rushing to become legal establishments.

Saloons were quickly reopened as taverns, bars, clubs, and cafés. All were regulated by state law; there was no federal regulation of the liquor industry. The liquor trade returned to the hands of private industry.

President Roosevelt also declared that tax on liquor should not be set so high as to keep violation of the law profitable, thereby keeping bootlegging alive. Prices would be made low enough that a black market for liquor would be unnecessary. He also allowed foreign liquor importation in an effort to drive down

On December 5, 1933, President Roosevelt signs the proclamation that announced the Twenty-first Amendment as law, ending Prohibition.

liquor prices through competition. The president hoped these steps would ensure that liquor was honestly produced, sold, and taxed.

The WONPR Disbands

In four and a half years, the WONPR had accomplished its goals. On November 8, 1933, Mrs. Sabin issued the following statement:

The Women's Organization for National Prohibition Reform was organized for and has given its support to three principles: first, the Repeal of the Eighteenth Amendment; second, the restoration to each state of its former power to regulate the manufacture, sale and transportation of intoxicating beverages within its own limits; third, that the resolution for Repeal of the Eighteenth Amendment should be submitted to conventions in several states rather than to the legislatures thereof.

Therefore when on December 5th, the thirty-sixth state in convention ratifies the Amendment repealing the Eighteenth Amendment, the Women's Organization for National Prohibition Reform will be dissolved.

I know I am speaking for all our members when I state that as good citizens we will continue as individuals to en-courage and support only such measures for control of liquor in our respective states as will promote temperance, law and order.[78]

Shortly before repeal had occurred the *Herald Tribune* remarked: "Mrs. Sabin's organization has developed many potential women leaders, whose talents for working in the cause of good government should continue to find expression after Prohibition Repeal has been won."[79]

The public did not want the organization to disband; many felt it should turn its attention to other worthy causes. The WONPR had proved itself worthy of the task it had undertaken. It had proved to the country that women could function effectively in the political arena. Sabin's Women had helped change history.

America in Recovery

With a new president at the helm, the country faced sweeping changes designed to speed economic recovery. Roosevelt's New Deal was quickly put into action. Its purpose was threefold: to effect permanent reform in the management of banks and stock exchanges, to supply relief to the needy, and to promote recovery through public programs such as the Public Works Administration by providing jobs on roads, dams, public buildings, and other federal projects.

The return of the liquor tax aided economic recovery by pumping millions of dollars back into the federal government, but many problems still remained. The failure of Prohibition, and the crime and corruption during the era, had shattered the faith of the people in political leaders and in the judicial and legislative systems.

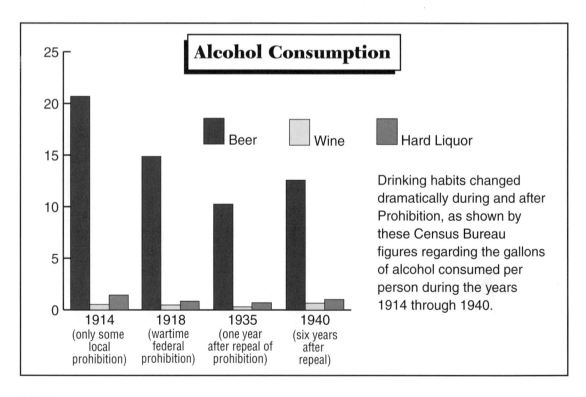

Alcohol Consumption

Beer   Wine   Hard Liquor

1914 (only some local prohibition)
1918 (wartime federal prohibition)
1935 (one year after repeal of prohibition)
1940 (six years after repeal)

Drinking habits changed dramatically during and after Prohibition, as shown by these Census Bureau figures regarding the gallons of alcohol consumed per person during the years 1914 through 1940.

Agents demonstrate how two smugglers (far left and far right) hid bottles of tequila in a gasoline tank, which was then filled with gas. After Prohibition was repealed, bootleggers often took up other illegal activities, such as gambling and extortion.

Crime Remains

It had been expected that after repeal bootleggers, and the crimes associated with them, would disappear. In reality, bootleggers merely turned to other criminal venues, infiltrating unions, gambling businesses, and extortion rackets. The organizational skills gangsters learned during Prohibition were put to use when they sought new sources of illegal income. Gangs and gangsters remained a very real problem. Those who supported repeal be-

lieving it would eliminate criminal activity were disappointed.

Repeal was most keenly appreciated by those who had addressed the problem as a moral issue. Individual freedom had been restored to the citizens. The president of Columbia University during that time compared the Eighteenth Amendment to the mid-1800s Fugitive Slave Law, which had bolstered slavery by declaring slaves the property of slave owners: "My own feeling toward Prohibition is exactly the feeling which my parents and my grandparents had toward slavery. I look upon the

Volstead Act precisely as they looked upon the Fugitive Slave Law. . . . The issue is one of plain, simple unadorned morality."[80]

The Volstead Act had set a precedent of nationwide government regulation of a single issue. The morality of this action, and of government regulation of drugs and other intoxicants, is still being debated today.

AA Is Founded

Some good came out of the Prohibition years. Numerous studies on the effects of alcohol had been conducted during Prohibition, increasing understanding of the addictive qualities of alcohol. Volunteer efforts to combat the problem through education rather than regulation were enhanced. Alcoholics Anonymous was founded in 1935 in Akron, Ohio, by Bill Wilson. Its goal was to give alcoholics the courage and knowledge needed to control their behavior and adopt abstinence. It was the first comprehensive organization to address the problems of alcoholics and to offer guidance on a continuing basis. This organization is still very active today and has helped millions of people overcome their addiction to alcohol.

Freedom to Drink Restricted Today

Local control of alcoholic beverages remains, and prohibition exists, in effect, primarily in rural areas with strong religious influence. In many cities across the country, the sale of alcoholic beverages is restricted on Sundays or between certain hours of the day. Many communities also ban liquor advertising. Television advertising of hard liquor is prohibited. These restrictions are controversial to many who are afraid history may be repeating itself. The question of whether prohibition in any form really works is widely contested. The *New Statesman* magazine of July 18, 1997, discussed this in an article called "The Perils of Prohibition":

> When it comes to the hunting of foxes and the consumption of tobacco and alcohol (not to mention the now settled question of the ownership of pistols or the under-debated prohibition of other drugs) ministers must face the twin tests of prohibition with honesty: will banning the advertising of tobacco result in less consumption of it or in better services to rescue users from their addiction? Or will it simply make abstainers feel better? Has the sustained prohibition of illicit drugs curbed or promoted their consumption? Will the outlawing of the hunting with hounds of other mammals result in less cruelty to the hunted or not? Or do we merely wish to ban that for which we, personally, do not have the taste? Each question requires a lengthier argument in its own right, but these are the questions politicians must ask before they act.[81]

Controversy also still surrounds the issue of whether restricting alcohol and other mood-altering substances intensifies their harmful effects. Journalist Richard Cowen contends that it does, labeling the phenomenon "the Iron Law of Prohibition." An article in *USA Today* magazine explains his theory:

The more intense the law enforcement, the more potent the prohibited substance becomes. When drugs or alcoholic beverages are prohibited, they will become more potent, have greater variability in potency, be adulterated with unknown or dangerous substances, and will not be produced and consumed under normal market constraints. The Iron Law undermines the prohibitionist case and reduces or outweighs the benefits ascribed to a decrease in consumption.[82]

Related problems have surfaced in many nations that have experimented with prohibition practices in varying degrees.

As recently as the 1980s, the Soviet Union tried to combat serious alcohol abuse in its population by raising prices and restricting sales of alcohol. These attempts failed for lack of public support. No successful or popular modern-day prohibition effort can be documented.

Politically Correct Propaganda

The U.S. government and special-interest groups continue to combat the use of alcohol and drugs through various programs and propaganda efforts similar to methods

---

Reflections from the College Campus

The experience of Prohibition is reflected in attitudes and concerns of people today. Restrictions of drinking laws are still hotly contested by the younger generation, as noted in Josh Friedman's article entitled, "We Don't Need No Prohibition," from the University Wire *of October 6, 1997.*

"Prohibition didn't work when the whole country tried it. People continued to drink, but they were forced to deal with smugglers and criminals. This development not only provided organized crime with a tremendous source of power but undermined the average person's respect for the law. When the law doesn't comport with common-sense or acceptable behavior, it gives citizens no reason to follow it.

So too with the current underage drinking laws. Passed in a fit of pique by (Ronald) Reagan's moralistic 'majority' and fortified by threats to terminate federal highway funds for states that didn't comply, the 21-year-old drinking age is prohibition of the worse sort. Both hypocritical (you can die for your country but not have a beer) and unsuccessful (look at any fraternity party), the current drinking age merely forces many students to drink surreptitiously, and thus unsafely."

used during the twenties: pamphlets warning of the dangers of drinking, lobbying for more police action and stricter legislation, and pressuring the liquor industry to pay for responsible drinking ads. The government distributes millions of dollars to antidrug and alcohol programs sponsored by groups ranging from the police to the Girl Scouts.

One special-interest group, Mothers Against Drunk Driving (MADD), formed in California in 1980 to persuade lawmakers there to enact more rigorous punishment for drunk driving. MADD is now a national organization with more than 320 local chapters across the country and boasting more than 600,000 donors and volunteers that raise millions of dollars for its cause.

Pressure from MADD and related organizations has yielded results. In August 1984, Congress appropriated $5.2 billion for the Transportation Department's interstate highway construction program but attached a rider denying millions of dollars to states that failed to raise the legal drinking age to twenty-one. By 1990, all states had complied. The liquor industry was both stunned and angry, claiming a partial form of prohibition had taken place with taxpayers' money used as a threat.

A Time of Human Suffering

H. L. Mencken, American journalist and social critic during the Prohibition era, wrote after the repeal of the Eighteenth Amendment:

> Prohibition went into effect on January 16, 1920, and blew up at last on

Drinking and Substance Abuse of Illegal Drugs

Another much contested debate concerns drinking and its relation to other substance abuse. The question remains whether drinking leads to other drugs or provides an outlet so that other drugs are not sought after. Mark Thorton explores what transpired during Prohibition days in his USA Today *article entitled, "Prohibition's Failure: Lessons for Today."*

"Although consumption of alcohol fell at the beginning of Prohibition, it subsequently increased. Alcohol became more dangerous to consume; crime burgeoned and became "organized"; the court and prison systems were stretched to the breaking point; and corruption of public officials was rampant. No measurable gains were made in productivity or in reduced absenteeism. Prohibition removed a significant source of tax revenue and greatly increased government spending. It led many drinkers to switch to opium, marijuana, patent medicines, cocaine, and other dangerous substances they would have been unlikely to use otherwise."

Certain groups, such as MADD (Mothers Against Drunk Driving), still wield considerable anti-alcohol power. Due to MADD's lobbying, by 1990 all states had raised the drinking age to twenty-one.

December 5, 1933—an elapsed time of twelve years, ten months and nineteen days. It seemed almost a geologic epoch while it was going on, and the human suffering that it entailed must have been a fair match for that of the Black Death or the Thirty Years War.[83]

This exaggerated view reflects an essential truth. Prohibition was a time of great turmoil in our country's history. The "noble experiment" failed ignobly, highlighting the nation's weaknesses, troubles, and conflicts before the world. Only through repeal did recovery begin, allowing the nation's strength to shine again.

Notes

Introduction: A Nation Divided

1. Daniel Cohen, *Prohibition: America Makes Alcohol Illegal.* Brookfield, CT: Millbrook Press, 1995, p. 52.

2. Quoted in Edward Behr, *Prohibition: Thirteen Years That Changed America.* New York: Arcade Publishing, 1996, p. 82.

3. Quoted in Behr, *Prohibition*, p. 150.

Chapter 1: The Roots of Prohibition

4. Quoted in Fletcher Dobyns, *The Amazing Story of Repeal.* Chicago: Signal Press, 1974, p. 233.

5. Quoted in Dobyns, *The Amazing Story of Repeal*, p. 228.

6. Quoted in Dobyns, *The Amazing Story of Repeal*, p. 227.

7. Quoted in Cohen, *Prohibition*, p. 26.

8. Quoted in Dobyns, *The Amazing Story of Repeal*, p. 237.

9. Quoted in Behr, *Prohibition*, p. 69.

10. Quoted in Behr, *Prohibition*, p. 78.

11. Quoted in Malcolm F. Willoughby, *Rum War at Sea.* Washington, DC: United States Coast Guard, 1964, p. 9.

12. Quoted in Behr, *Prohibition*, p. 82.

13. Quoted in Behr, *Prohibition*, p. 80.

Chapter 2: "Tell 'em Joe Sent You"

14. Quoted in Henry Lee, *How Dry We Were: Prohibition Revisited.* Englewood Cliffs, NJ: Prentice-Hall, 1963, p. 6.

15. Quoted in Paul Sann, *The Lawless Decade.* New York: Crown, 1967, p. 191.

16. Quoted in Lee, *How Dry We Were*, p. 58.

17. Quoted in Time-Life Book Editors, *This Fabulous Century: 1920–1930.* Alexandria, VA: Time-Life Books, 1969, p. 160.

18. Quoted in Sann, *The Lawless Decade*, p. 191.

19. Quoted in Lee, *How Dry We Were*, p. 76.

20. Quoted in Lee, *How Dry We Were*, p. 74.

21. Quoted in Cohen, *Prohibition*, p. 42.

22. Quoted in Dobyns, *The Amazing Story of Repeal*, p. 56.

Chapter 3: Rumrunners

23. Quoted in Behr, *Prohibition*, p. 133.

24. Quoted in C. H. Gervais, *Rumrunners.* Scarborough, Ontario, Canada: Firefly Books, 1980, p. 45.

25. Quoted in Gervais, *Rumrunners*, p. 29.

26. Quoted in Lee, *How Dry We Were*, p. 109.

27. Behr, *Prohibition*, p. 134.

28. Quoted in Behr, *Prohibition*, p. 137.

29. Lee, *How Dry We Were*, p. 96.

30. Quoted in Lee, *How Dry We Were*, p. 110.

31. Quoted in Behr, *Prohibition*, p. 142.

32. Quoted in John Kobler, *Ardent Spirits.* New York: G. P. Putnam's Sons, 1973, p. 255.

Chapter 4: Chicago: Corruption, Crime, and Capone

33. Quoted in Henry Steele Commager, ed., *The American Destiny: The Twenties.* London: Orbis, 1986, p. 61.

34. Quoted in Behr, *Prohibition*, p. 181.

35. Quoted in Behr, *Prohibition*, p. 181.

36. Quoted in Dobyns, *The Amazing Story of Repeal*, p. 373.

37. Quoted in Andrew Sinclair, *Prohibition: The Era of Excess.* Boston: Little, Brown, 1962, p. 227.

38. Quoted in Carl Sifakis, *The Mafia Encyclopedia.* New York: Facts On File, 1987, p. 323.

39. Quoted in Laurence Bergreen, *Capone: The Man and the Era.* New York: Simon and Schuster, 1994, p. 403.

40. Quoted in Time-Life Book Editors, *This Fabulous Century*, p. 174.

41. Quoted in Bergreen, *Capone*, p. 346.

42. Quoted in Sifakis, *The Mafia Encyclopedia*, p. 73.

43. Quoted in Sifakis, *The Mafia Encyclopedia*, p. 289.

44. Quoted in Sifakis, *The Mafia Encyclopedia*, p. 289.

Chapter 5: President Harding and the Ohio Gang

45. Quoted in Commager, *The American Destiny*, p. 21.

46. Quoted in Behr, *Prohibition*, p. 113.

47. Quoted in Behr, *Prohibition*, p. 114.

48. Quoted in Isabel Leighton, ed., *The Aspirin Age*. New York: Simon and Schuster, 1949, p. 93.

49. Quoted in Commager, *The American Destiny*, p. 27.

50. Quoted in Sinclair, *Prohibition*, p. 259.

51. Quoted in Sinclair, *Prohibition*, p. 252.

52. Quoted in Commager, *The American Destiny*, p. 28.

53. Quoted in Behr, *Prohibition*, p. 106.

Chapter 6: The Country in Turmoil

54. Quoted in Behr, *Prohibition*, p. 162.

55. Quoted in Behr, *Prohibition*, p. 172.

56. Quoted in Kobler, *Ardent Spirits*, p. 234.

57. Quoted in Kobler, *Ardent Spirits*, p. 224.

58. Quoted in Behr, *Prohibition*, p. 222.

59. Quoted in Kobler, *Ardent Spirits*, p. 274.

60. Quoted in Sinclair, *Prohibition*, p. 189.

61. Quoted in Lee, *How Dry We Were*, p. 165.

62. Quoted in Kobler, *Ardent Spirits*, p. 236.

63. Quoted in Kobler, *Ardent Spirits*, p. 341.

64. Quoted in Sinclair, *Prohibition*, p. 354.

65. Quoted in Kobler, *Ardent Spirits*, p. 351.

66. Quoted in Behr, *Prohibition*, p. 234.

67. Quoted in Lee, *How Dry We Were*, p. 229.

68. Quoted in Lee, *How Dry We Were*, p. 236.

Chapter 7: Women and Repeal

69. Quoted in Dobyns, *The Amazing Story of Repeal*, p. 3.

70. Quoted in Commager, *The American Destiny*, p. 64.

71. Quoted in Kobler, *Ardent Spirits*, p. 342.

72. Grace C. Root, *Women and Repeal*. New York: Harper and Brothers, 1934, p. 10.

73. Quoted in Root, *Women and Repeal*, p. 13.

74. Quoted in Root, *Women and Repeal*, p. 34.

75. Quoted in Root, *Women and Repeal*, p. 39.

76. Quoted in Root, *Women and Repeal*, p. 44.

77. Quoted in Root, *Women and Repeal*, p. 74.

78. Quoted in Root, *Women and Repeal*, p. 158.

79. Quoted in Root, *Women and Repeal*, p. 157.

Epilogue: America in Recovery

80. Quoted in Commager, *The American Destiny*, p. 64.

81. Quoted in "The Perils of Prohibition," *New Statesman*, July 18, 1997.

82. Mark Thorton, "Prohibition's Failure: Lessons for Today," *USA Today*, March 1992, pp. 70–73.

83. Quoted in Behr, *Prohibition*, p. 238.

For Further Reading

Frederick Lewis Allen, *Only Yesterday: An Informal History of the Nineteen Twenties.* New York: Harper, 1931. Excellent source of photographs and general information of the era.

James P. Barry, *The Noble Experiment.* New York: Franklin Watts, 1972. Good overview with several chapters detailing gangland crime.

Donald Barr Chidsey, *On and Off the Wagon.* New York: Cowles, 1969. Comprehensive overview of Prohibition.

Daniel Cohen, *Prohibition: America Makes Alcohol Illegal.* Brookfield, CT: Millbrook Press, 1995. An easy-to-read overview of Prohibition and its roots in America.

Arnold Madison, *Carry Nation.* Nashville: Nelson, 1977. Interesting biography of this unique woman.

Margaret Sharman, *Take Ten Years: 1920's.* Austin, TX: Raintree Steck-Vaughn, 1993. Topics and people of the decade that made news headlines.

Leslie Waller, *The Mob: The Story of Organized Crime in America.* New York: Delacorte, 1973. In-depth account of the history of organized crime.

Works Consulted

Books

Edward Behr, *Prohibition: Thirteen Years That Changed America*. New York: Arcade Publishing, 1996. A well-documented, up-to-date account of Prohibition.

Laurence Bergreen, *Capone: The Man and the Era*. New York: Simon and Schuster, 1994. A detailed biography of the gangster most closely associated with Prohibition.

Henry Steele Commager, ed., *The American Destiny: The Twenties*. London: Orbis, 1986. A pictorial history of the decade with a lengthy and informative chapter devoted to issues and events of Prohibition.

Clarence Darrow and Victor S. Yarros, *The Prohibition Mania*. New York: Boni and Liveright, 1927. The prominent authors offer their personal, contemporary response to the issue.

Fletcher Dobyns, *The Amazing Story of Repeal*. Chicago: Signal Press, 1974. Excellent account of the mechanics of repeal and of the propaganda prevalent at that time.

C. H. Gervais, *The Rumrunners*. Scarborough, Ontario, Canada: Firefly Books, 1980. Pictures and personal accounts covering the illegal liquor trade.

John Kobler, *Ardent Spirits*. New York: G. P. Putnam's Sons, 1973. Excellent source of detailed information on the temperance movement and history leading up to Prohibition years.

Henry Lee, *How Dry We Were: Prohibition Revisited*. Englewood Cliffs, NJ: Prentice-Hall, 1963. Detailed and information-packed book on all aspects of Prohibition.

Isabel Leighton, ed., *The Aspirin Age*. New York: Simon and Schuster, 1949. A thorough collection of profiles on famous people and events by authors, circa 1919–1941.

Robert K. Murray, *The Politics of Normalcy*. New York: Norton, 1973. An in-depth examination of Warren Harding's political philosophy.

Grace C. Root, *Women and Repeal*. New York: Harper and Brothers, 1934. Excellent source covering the women's organization that spearheaded the call for repeal.

Paul Sann, *The Lawless Decade*. New York: Crown, 1967. A pictorial history of the times providing much information on people as well as events.

Carl Sifakis, *The Mafia Encyclopedia*. New York: Facts On File, 1987. An excellent, alphabetically arranged, reference collection of biographies and issues relating to organized crime including many crime bosses of the Prohibition era.

Andrew Sinclair, *Prohibition: The Era of Excess*. Boston: Little, Brown, 1962. Good overview of Prohibition with excellent section detailing repeal.

Mark Sullivan and Dan Rather, *Our Times*. New York: Scribner, 1996. Social history of the country from the turn of the century through the 1920s.

Time-Life Book Editors, *This Fabulous Century: 1920–1930*. Alexandria, VA: Time-Life Books, 1969. Full pictorial account of people, places, politics, fads, and fashions of the decade.

Eugene P. Trani and David L. Wilson, *The Presidency of Warren G. Harding*. Lawrence: University Press of Kansas, 1977. A comprehensive account of the president and his administration.

Malcolm F. Willoughby, *Rum War at Sea*. Washington, DC: United States Coast Guard, 1964. Informative account of the role the Coast Guard played in enforcing Prohibition laws and fighting illegal liquor traffic.

Magazines

New Statesman, July 18, 1997. "The Perils of Prohibition." Article focusing on the banning of illegal substances.

Sirs Digest, Spring 1996. "Temperance and Prohibition." A look at history leading up to and including the Prohibition years.

University Wire, October 6, 1997. Josh Friedman, "We Don't Need No Prohibition." A college student's view of Prohibition and related current issues.

USA Today, March 1992. Mark Thorton, "Prohibition's Failure: Lessons for Today." A hindsight view of why Prohibition failed and what it means to Americans today.

Index

Picture Credits

Cover photo: Hulton-Getty Picture Collection/Tony Stone Images

American Stock/Archive Photos, 84

Archive Photos, 9, 16, 28, 50, 52, 59, 78

Hayward and Blanche Cirker, *Dictionary of American Portraits*, Dover Publications, Inc., 1967, 67

Corbis-Bettmann, 11, 14, 15, 21, 24, 26 (right), 31, 37, 58, 61, 62, 63, 64

FPG International, 10, 27, 34, 39, 68, 77, 79, 95

Franklin D. Roosevelt Presidential Library, 90

Library of Congress, 73

Lineworks, Inc., 18

New York Times Co./Archive Photos, 41, 47

Prints Old & Rare, 86

UPI/Corbis-Bettmann, 19, 26 (left), 29, 30, 32, 33, 36, 44, 48, 49, 51, 53, 54, 60, 66, 71, 72, 74, 75, 80, 82, 88, 92, 99

About the Author

Renee C. Rebman has published seventeen plays for community theater and high school productions. Her one-act drama *Play Ball*, the story of Toni Stone, the first woman to play baseball in the Negro American League, has been placed in the library of the National Baseball Hall of Fame in Cooperstown, New York. Many of her plays are historical dramatizations. Her love of history and research led her to write young adult nonfiction.

Rebman also enjoys speaking at writers' conferences and acting and directing in community theater, and she is an active volunteer at local elementary schools.

Rebman lives in Lexington, Ohio, with her daughter, Scarlett, and her son, Roddy.